NEW TESTAMENT GUIDES

General Editor
A.T. Lincoln

1 CORINTHIANS

1 CORINTHIANS

James D.G. Dunn

Sheffield Academic Press

Copyright © 1995 Sheffield Academic Press

Published by Sheffield Academic Press Ltd
Mansion House
19 Kingfield Road
Sheffield, S11 9AS
England

Printed on acid-free paper in Great Britain
by The Cromwell Press
Melksham, Wiltshire

British Library Cataloguing in Publication Data

A catalogue record for this book is available
from the British Library

ISBN 1-85075-742-9

Contents

Acknowledgments

I wish to express my appreciation to the members of the New Testament Postgraduate Seminar, including especially my colleagues Stephen Barton and Loren Stuckenbruck. The seminar's programme for 1994–95 was 1 Corinthians and the weekly meetings helped me shape the structure and content of the following chapters. The book is dedicated to the members of the Seminar with thanks for the stimulus and enjoyment provided.

Abbreviations

AB	Anchor Bible
BNTC	Black's New Testament Commentaries
CBQ	*Catholic Biblical Quarterly*
HTR	*Harvard Theological Review*
IB	Interpreter's Bible
ICC	International Critical Commentary
Int	*Interpretation*
JBL	*Journal of Biblical Literature*
JRH	*Journal of Religious History*
JSJ	*Journal for the Study of Judaism in the Persian, Hellenistic and Roman Period*
JSNT	*Journal for the Study of the New Testament*
JSNTSup	*Journal for the Study of the New Testament, Supplement Series*
JTS	*Journal of Theological Studies*
MeyerK	H.A.W. Meyer (ed.), Kritisch-exegetischer Kommentar über das Neue Testament
MNTC	Moffatt NT Commentary
NCB	New Century Bible
NICNT	New International Commentary on the New Testament
NovT	*Novum Testamentum*
NovTSup	*Novum Testamentum* Supplements
NTS	*New Testament Studies*
SBLDS	SBL Dissertation Series
SBT	Studies in Biblical Theology
TDNT	G. Kittel and G. Friedrich (eds.), *Theological Dictionary of the New Testament*
TNTC	Tyndale New Testament Commentaries
TynBul	*Tyndale Bulletin*
WUNT	Wissenschaftliche Untersuchungen zum Neuen Testament

1

INTRODUCTION

1 CORINTHIANS IS OF PARTICULAR INTEREST to the student of the
New Testament. For one thing, as my old teacher William
Barclay used to say, it takes the lid off a New Testament
church in a way that no other writing does. We begin to see
how Christianity established itself and what it meant to be
Christian, to be the church in a Mediterranean city in the
middle of the first century. It's a fascinating picture, one very
far removed from the ideal of the pure New Testament
church which still influences many people's thinking about
New Testament Christianity. But that only increases the
fascination of the letter. For it soon becomes clear from even
a casual reading of the letter that the church in Corinth was
a very mixed group, with several differing views and practices which put considerable strains on their common life. So
much so that one soon begins to wonder how it was that they
held together at all as a church.

Not least of the fascination is the way in which Paul dealt
with these tensions. And since the letter was preserved, to be
acknowledged as canonical in due course, we may assume
that its handling of these tensions was recognized to be of
lasting value. The potential benefit of a close study of the
letter is therefore considerable.

The other interesting aspect of 1 Corinthians is that it has
attracted an amazing amount of attention over the past few
years. Precisely because it deals with so many practical
issues of mutual relations within a first-century church and
between its members and their neighbours in a first-century
city, and is not simply a theological treatise or all purpose

ethical exhortation, the letter invites a variety of approaches. Over this century, therefore, 1 Corinthians has been in effect a testing ground for different hermeneutical techniques and theories. Indeed, one can almost trace the rise (and decline) of such theories by reference to 1 Corinthians and how they have fared in explaining the features of that letter. We shall see this to be the case with the history of religions approach from the beginning of the century, and with the more recent application of the social sciences and of literary and rhetorical analysis to New Testament documents. The fact that two rather diverse contemporary movements, Christian feminism and charismatic renewal, find themselves equally caught up in the interpretation of 1 Corinthians confirms the amazingly contemporary relevance of the letter.

1 Corinthians is evidently a letter, then, which will repay careful study, both for information about Christian beginnings, in the practice it will provide for use of different tools of interpretation, and for its potential continuing theological and ecclesiological value.

But how to proceed?

Since the letter is so clearly structured into a sequence of topics it would perhaps be simplest if we took them one at a time. In fact, however, the topics tend to fall into coherent groups. This is partly because Paul (and/or the reports he received from Corinth) ordered them in a natural sequence (1–4, factionalism in the church at Corinth; 5–10, the church's external relations; 11–14, its internal relations; 15, the resurrection from the dead; 16.1-4, the collection). These groupings in turn have tended to attract different waves of scholarly interest and so reflect in a measure the developments and shifts in scholarship on 1 Corinthians. It is possible therefore to proceed by combining a more or less orderly progression through the topics dealt with in 1 Corinthians, with a description of the various trends in study of the letter through the present century. Other underlying themes (Paul's own authority and the theological ground of his claims) run through the letter as a whole and require separate treatment.

A major concern of what follows is to give students some indication and sample of the secondary literature which has grown up around this letter, including some of the classic treatments as well as more recent discussions. As with so many New Testament writings, however, the secondary literature has become vast, marked in recent years by a steadily rising curve of publications in which, unfortunately, quantity often outstrips quality. The treatment perforce has had to be selective and inevitably arbitrary, but the intention has been to give a representative sweep of the diverse contributions which have been made towards shedding more (or less) light on the exegesis and interpretation of 1 Corinthians. Since original suggestions and insights tend to come in monographs and special articles rather than in commentaries (whose function is more directed to the survey of such contributions) in what follows more attention is given to the former than to the latter.

But first it would be as well to clear away some preliminary questions which help set the scene and enable us to 'lift the lid' off the church in Corinth more effectively.

Recommendations for Further Reading

More weighty and detailed:

C.K. Barrett, *A Commentary on the First Epistle to the Corinthians* (BNTC; London: A. & C. Black, 1971).

H. Conzelmann, *1 Corinthians* (Hermeneia; Philadelphia: Fortress, 1975).

G.D. Fee, *The First Epistle to the Corinthians* (NICNT; Grand Rapids: Eerdmans, 1987).

J. Héring, *The First Epistle of Saint Paul to the Corinthians* (London: Hodder & Stoughton, 1974).

J. Moffatt, *The First Epistle of Paul to the Corinthians* (MNTC; London: Hodder & Stoughton, 1938).

A. Robertson and A. Plummer, *The First Epistle of St Paul to the Corinthians* (ICC; Edinburgh T.& T. Clark, 1914).

J. Weiss, *Der erste Korintherbrief* (MeyerK; Göttingen: Vandenhoeck & Ruprecht, 1910), one of the great commentaries of this century.

Less weighty and more accessible:

W. Barclay, *The Letters to the Corinthians* (Edinburgh: St Andrews Press, 1956).

F.F. Bruce, *1 and 2 Corinthians* (NCB; Edinburgh: Oliphants, 1971).

C.T. Craig, *The First Epistle to the Corinthians* (IB; New York: Abingdon, 1953).

M.A. Getty, *First Corinthians, Second Corinthians* (Collegeville, MN: Liturgical Press, 1983).

F.W. Grosheide, *Commentary on the First Epistle to the Corinthians* (NICNT; Grand Rapids: Eerdmans, 1953).

R.A. Harrisville, *1 Corinthians* (Minneapolis: Augsburg, 1987).

L. Morris, *The First Epistle of Paul to the Corinthians* (TNTC; Leicester: InterVarsity Press, 2nd edn, 1985).

J. Murphy-O'Connor, *1 Corinthians* (Wilmington: Glazier, 1979).

W.F. Orr and J. A. Walther, *1 Corinthians* (AB; Garden City, NY: Doubleday, 1976).

K. Quast, *Reading the Corinthian Correspondence: An Introduction* (New York: Paulist Press, 1994).

J. Ruef, *Paul's First Letter to Corinth* (Pelican Commentary; Harmondsworth: Penguin, 1971).

C.H. Talbert, *Reading Corinthians: A Literary and Theological Commentary on 1 and 2 Corinthians* (New York: Crossroad, 1989).

M.E. Thrall, *The First and Second Letter of Paul to the Corinthians* (Cambridge Bible Commentary; Cambridge University Press, 1965).

B. Witherington, *Conflict and Community in Corinth: A Socio-Rhetorical Commentary* (Grand Rapids: Eerdmans, 1994).

2

PRELIMINARY QUESTIONS

Author and Date

WE CAN BE MORE CONFIDENT over these preliminary matters than with almost any other ancient writing from this period, New Testament or otherwise. There is no dispute to speak of regarding the *author*. For example, 1 Corinthians has the kind of attestation of which most students of ancient texts can only dream. One of the earliest post-New Testament writings, *1 Clement* (usually dated to the late first century), is addressed to the same church, and explicitly calls upon its readers to 'Take up the epistle of the blessed Paul the apostle...With true inspiration he charged you concerning himself and Cephas and Apollos, because even then you had made yourselves partisans' (*1 Clem.* 47.1-3). The reference to 1 Corinthians is beyond dispute; to have such a clear cross-reference within about 40 years of the first letter is highly unusual. So firmly is 1 Corinthians linked to Paul that even if we did not have the account in Acts we would have to assume that the Paul of 1 Corinthians was the founder of the church in Corinth.

Moreover, the degree of correlation between the letter itself and the account in Acts of Paul's dealings with the church in Corinth is sufficient to establish our confidence in the Acts account. Not only does Acts confirm that Paul was the founder of the Corinthian church (Acts 18.1-11), but it confirms also the subsequent important role of Apollos in the development of the church (cf. Acts 18.27–19.1 with 1 Cor. 3.5-10). We might also note the correlation between Acts and

1 Corinthians regarding Paul's other associates including Timothy (Acts 18.5; 19.22; 1 Cor. 4.17; 16.10) and Priscilla and Aquila (Acts 18.2, 18; 1 Cor. 16.19)—though whether the appearance of a Sosthenes in both Acts 18.17 ('ruler of the synagogue') and 1 Cor. 1.1 is more than a coincidence is hard to tell. At all events we can draw on Acts to fill in the background to 1 Corinthians with greater confidence than is often the case.

This is important particularly as regards the *date* of the letter. For two of the firmest dates used to plot the course of Paul's mission are derived from the Acts account of Paul's mission in Corinth. The first is the reference to the expulsion of the Jews from Rome by the Emperor Claudius. According to Acts 18.2, Paul met Priscilla and Aquila in Corinth shortly after the latter had come from Italy as a result of Claudius's decree. This decree is usually and most likely to be dated to 49, which suggests in turn that Paul arrived in Corinth in about 50 ce. The second date is given by the reference to Gallio as Roman proconsul of Achaia (Acts 18.12-17). A fragmentary inscription enables us to date Gallio's term of office probably from 51/52 (see Murphy-O'Connor, *Paul's Corinth*, pp. 149-60, 178-82). Once again the degree to which these two points of external evidence correlate with the account in Acts is impressive. For according to Acts 18.11 and 18 Paul's stay in Corinth lasted at least eighteen months, and that period very neatly spans the effective period between the two dates. In other words, we can assume with an amazing degree of confidence that the church in Corinth was established during Paul's time in Corinth, that is in the period 50–52 ce (see e.g. Jewett).

The letter itself presupposes some elapse of time since Paul's departure. After a visit back to Antioch (according to Acts 18.22) Paul had returned to the Aegean and made his base in Ephesus (Acts 19.8-10). During that period Apollos had arrived in Corinth, had conducted a substantial ministry there and had then also moved on (1 Cor. 16.12). Paul had written an earlier letter (1 Cor. 5.9) which is now almost certainly lost. And there had been some coming and going between Paul and Corinth, presumably across the Aegean (between Ephesus and Corinth)—Timothy (1 Cor. 4.17),

Apollos (1 Cor. 16.12), Sosthenes (? 1 Cor. 1.1), Chloe's people
(1 Cor. 1.11) and another Corinthian delegation consisting of
Stephanas, Fortunatus and Achaicus (1 Cor. 16.17), probably
bringing with them a letter from the church in Corinth
(1 Cor. 7.1). We must return to some of these details below,
but for the moment we may note how they all build up to the
probable conclusion that 1 Corinthians was written in the
period 54–55 CE. Establishing the precise date, however, is of
less importance than setting 1 Corinthians in context and
determining its role in the sequence of Paul's dealings with
Corinth.

Corinth and the Evidence from Archaeology

Before focusing on the letter itself, it is worth pausing to note
a number of details relating to Corinth and its customs
which have bearing on the letter and on our interpretation of
it. An intriguing feature of the letter is that because it is so
concerned with social relationships within the city, information regarding Corinth and the customs of the time
(including the evidence of archaeology) can help fill out the
context of the various issues dealt with in the letter. Some
points I will simply mention here and draw upon more fully
later on when dealing with particular issues. Fuller details
on what follows can be found in introductions to the major
commentaries and in Murphy-O'Connor (*Paul's Corinth* and
'Corinth').

Corinth had been re-established as a Roman colony in
44 BCE. Its location on the isthmus linking the Peloponnese
to the rest of Greece, with a newly dug canal linking the Gulf
of Corinth to the Aegean, made it a natural crossroads for
north–south and east–west traffic, the voyage round the
southern end of the Peloponnese (Cape Maleae) being notori-
ously dangerous. Given the vigour of the new colonists,
mainly freedmen, the city could hardly fail to succeed. Even
from this brief description we can already draw some
pointers which may influence interpretation of 1 Corinthians.

In particular as a political, commercial and financial centre
Corinth numbered some very wealthy men among its citizens.
We need to bear this in mind when we read that 'not many

[of the Corinthian believers] were powerful, not many were of noble birth' (1 Cor. 1.26). By chance archaeology has turned up the name of one of these few well-to-do Corinthian Christians, since an inscription attributing a pavement laid in mid-first century ce to Erastus 'at his own expense' quite likely refers to the Erastus, 'the city treasurer', mentioned in Rom. 16.23 (Romans having been written from Corinth). Ironically, of course, archaeology can only provide such correlation for those financially capable of leaving such monuments behind. On another front we could note that the biennial Isthmian Games had been re-established about 50 years before Paul's first visit, something of which Paul could hardly be unaware when he dictated 1 Cor. 9.24-27 (he could have attended the games in 51 CE).

Archaeology has given us a remarkably clear picture of the city centre at the time of Paul. The prominence of the *bema*, the platform-like podium in the centre of the *agora* (market place) used for public proclamations and speeches, is a reminder of the importance of public speaking (rhetoric) in the ancient Greco-Roman city. In addition, evidence of numerous shrines dedicated to different gods (Apollo, Athena, Aphrodite, Asclepios, etc.) shows how religious the city was (cf. 1 Cor. 8.5, 'many gods and many lords'). Their public positioning also gives an insight into what must have been involved in 'eating in the temple of an idol' (8.10) and into the social pressures on the members of the Christian community to take part in such important social occasions (cf. 10.20-22). On the other hand, Corinth's reputation for moral laxness ('to act like a Corinthian' = to fornicate) comes from a much earlier period and may owe more to Athenian rivalry than anything else (just as venereal disease used to be called 'the English pox' by the French and 'the French pox' by the English). The danger or enticement of moral laxity was probably no greater in Corinth than in other major commercial cities of the time.

How strong the Jewish community was we cannot tell, but according to the Jewish philosopher, Philo of Alexandria (an older contemporary of Paul's), Jewish colonies were scattered throughout Asia Minor and Greece (*Embassy to Gaius* 281), and given the character and location of the city we can assume a significant Jewish minority. This may be important, since according to Acts the church in Corinth began as a breakaway from the synagogue, and continued to be regarded by the Roman authorities as an intra-Jewish affair (Acts 18.4-8, 12-17). A broken lintel inscribed '[Syna]gogue of the Hebr[ews]' comes from a later period.

Archaeological evidence throws further light on 1 Corinthians in two ways. One is the numerous small shops uncovered as part of Corinth city centre at the time of Paul's visit. These provide a fair idea of the sort of conditions Paul would have enjoyed (or endured) when working to support himself in Corinth (1 Cor. 9.12, 15-18). Opening as they did straight on to market place or thoroughfare they must have afforded many an opportunity for contact and conversation (Murphy-O'Connor, *Paul's Corinth*, pp. 176-77). The meat market, important in the discussion of dining out (10.25), is referred to in two inscriptions (see Gill).

The other is the more widespread evidence of house size. This is important since the first churches all met in private homes. We know of two in Corinth—the church in the house of Prisca and Aquilla (1 Cor. 16.19) and, according to Rom. 16.23 (remembering again that Romans was almost certainly written from Corinth), 'the whole church [in Corinth]' met in the house of Gaius (presumably the Gaius of 1 Cor. 1.14). So archaeology can give us some idea of how large the church in Corinth could have been. We have, in fact, evidence regarding only one substantial villa from Corinth at the time of Paul, but also good evidence of a range of properties in Pompeii and Ostia (the port of Rome) from about the same period. The general impression of those who have studied the dimensions of these houses is that even well-to-do houses would have been hard pressed to accommodate more than about 40 people (Murphy-O'Connor, *Paul's Corinth*, p. 164). B. Blue argues that larger gatherings would have been possible (up to 100 people), but furnishings and statuary would have restricted space, partition walls would have limited effective use of adjoining rooms, and it would be unwise to assume that the Corinthian church had attracted any of the super rich (who might enjoy proconsular style mansions).

On present evidence, therefore, it would be wiser to

assume that 'the whole church' in Corinth to whom 1
Corinthians was written might have comprised no more than
about three or four dozen. At the very least, in assessing the
dynamics of opposition to Paul and of the social tensions in
the Corinthian church, we should bear in mind the likelihood
that the overall numbers were relatively small. And when we
add in the detail given in 14.23-24, that the gatherings of the
whole church were open to the unbeliever and outsider, the
resulting picture is of a dynamic and changing group.

1 Corinthians is thus a good example of the extent to
which the findings of archaeology can and should influence
the interpretation of an ancient or biblical text. Even if it is
only rarely that a particular archaeological artefact can illuminate a particular text, the more general illumination of the
place and period provided by both contemporary texts and
archaeological finds is bound to reflect beneficially on our
grasp of the issues dealt with in the letter and on our ability
to appreciate the force of the letter within its original
context.

The Occasion of the Letter

There is general agreement that 1 Corinthians was written
by Paul from Ephesus in response to information brought to
him by two sets of visitors, and possibly also Apollos himself
(16.12). It is also clear enough that the structure of the letter
is determined by the need to respond to issues put to Paul by
the two embassies.

The clearest indication comes in 7.1—'Now concerning the
matters about which you wrote'. A letter had evidently been
brought to Paul outlining certain questions or putting
forward a Corinthian viewpoint on a number of issues. As
already noted, the likelihood is that it had been brought by
the group referred to in 16.17—Stephanas, Fortunatus and
Achaicus. Paul's strong affirmation of them ('Give recognition
to such', 16.18) may imply that they were able to function
both as Paul's spokesmen and as emissaries of the
Corinthian church.

We are able to gain a clear idea of what was in the letter
brought by this group, for the subject matter of the letter is
introduced by a formula (*peri de*) which is then repeated in

1 Corinthians (7.25; 8.1; 12.1; 16.1, 12) as Paul evidently moves through a sequence of further topics. Since *peri de* is a formula Paul rarely uses elsewhere, the most obvious deduction (Hurd, pp. 63-65, but disputed by Mitchell, pp. 191-92) is that the sequence of topics ΄thus introduced in 1 Corinthians is the sequence of issues raised by the Corinthians' letter. In other words, the Corinthian letter probably put to Paul a series of questions and/or viewpoints on the following subjects and in the following order: (1) sexual relations between husband and wife (7.1-24), (2) the unmarried (7.25-40), (3) food offered to idols (8.1–11.1), (4) spiritual gifts (12.1–14.40), (5) the collection (16.1-4), and (6) Apollos (16.12).

The only passages which really disturb this analysis of the sequence of topics from 1 Corinthians 7 onwards are 11.2-34, on the veiling of women when they pray and prophesy and on selfish behaviour at the common meal, and ch. 15, on the resurrection of the dead. But it is obvious that the topics dealt with in these passages were quite as contentious as those introduced by the *peri de* formula. It could be that Paul simply omitted the *peri de* formula in these cases, as a stylistic variation. However, the allusion to oral reports in 11.18 and 15.12 suggests that the letter had not in fact raised these topics, but the Stephanas delegation had done so, probably on their own initiative. In which case several corollaries follow: (a) it was Paul's choice to slot his treatment of these topics into the sequence of the issues raised by the Corinthian letter; (b) we may guess that there had been insufficient concern or consensus in the Corinthian church about the need or desirability of putting these issues to Paul; and (c) Paul's commendation of the Stephanas delegation would include his approval of their initiative in apprising him of these further problems in the Corinthian assembly.

The other group of visitors were Chloe's people mentioned in 1.11. It is also clear that they had brought news of serious divisions and quarrels among the Corinthians (1.10-11). So serious were these reports that Paul evidently felt it necessary to deal with them immediately. This provides the subject matter of the first main section of the letter running through to the end of ch. 4. Chapters 5 and 6 are left somewhat awkwardly between the responses to these two sets of reports, but 5.1 clearly indicates that the subject matter (incest, immorality and one brother taking another to court) had also been reported (verbally) to Paul. So again we may assume that the subject matter had been reported orally to Paul by one or other of the two delegations. If by Chloe's people, that would explain why Paul dealt with it before turning to the Corinthian letter; if by the Stephanas group, that would imply that Paul thought this oral report was the most serious of the problems brought to him by the Stephanas group.

How far we can press behind this basic information is uncertain. The most ambitious and intriguing attempt to explain and reconstruct the course of events leading up to the letter itself has been that of John Hurd. He reckons on four stages in Paul's dialogue with the Corinthian church (1 Corinthians being the fourth). The first was Paul's founding mission. In this he may have himself discouraged marriage and sexual relations between married couples, may have preached that 'all things are lawful', and may have encouraged women's active participation in worship. Subsequently, however, Paul changed his mind (probably under the influence of the apostolic decree referred to in Acts 15.20 and 29) in order to facilitate relations between Jews and Gentiles in his churches, and wrote the previous letter (1 Cor. 5.9) which allowed marriage (to avoid immorality) but was otherwise more restrictive in its teaching. This caused confusion and resentment in Corinth, resulting in the letter which they wrote to him (1 Cor. 7.1) in which they posed the questions which Paul's own *volte-face* had raised for them, and in which they cited Paul's own earlier teaching against him. 1 Corinthians would then be Paul's attempt to justify his more mature judgment on these matters.

Of course, it is impossible to be sure of all that lies behind the letter in its present form. Hurd's attempt to explain as much as possible from within the letter itself without relying too heavily on hypotheses based on external evidence—while a bold and important endeavour—does leave out of consideration too many of the factors which we will consider in later chapters. Nevertheless the value of Hurd's thesis is its

reminder that the problems posed to Paul at Corinth may not
have been entirely on the Corinthians' side and may not have
been the result of them departing from some pristine
teaching of Paul or of later converts (through Apollos?)
corrupting Paul's original teaching. Apart from anything
else, the inference drawn from 1.12-16 (baptisms attributed
to Apollos and Cephas) has to be weighed against the inference of 4.15 and 9.2 that Paul claimed sole paternity and
apostolic rights in regard to the Corinthians as a whole.
Hurd reminds us that Paul himself may have developed and
changed/matured his teaching. As another example, we may
compare John Drane, who finds it necessary to hypothesize a
somewhat similar swinging back and forth in Paul's development as we trace it from Galatians through the Corinthian
letters to Romans.

Here again, the point is not whether Hurd and Drane are
right in the detail of their theses. It is rather that we must
remember how much Paul's theology and teaching must have
adapted and developed as new openings for and challenges to
his gospel and ideas of Christian community caused him to
formulate his insights as a theologian and missionary afresh.
More than any other of Paul's letters, 1 Corinthians indicates
how much of Paul's theology as we have it was contextually
conditioned. An exegesis which fails to ask whether and to
what extent Paul's language and emphases on particular
points were determined by the situation confronting him is
most likely to mistake Paul's point and miss its nuances and
overtones.

The Unity of the Letter

During the past century it has by no means always been
agreed that 1 Corinthians is a single letter. The starting
point has usually been the reference to the former letter in
5.9. Unwillingness to accept that it would have been allowed
to become lost resulted in a variety of attempts to find it
retained somewhere within the Corinthian correspondence.
An attractive suggestion for some has been that it was
preserved in 2 Cor. 6.14–7.1, which can plausibly be seen as
an awkward insertion in the context of 2 Corinthians 6–7.

But tensions within 1 Corinthians have encouraged attempts to trace elements of the former letter within 1 Corinthians itself. For example, the awkward transition from chs. 4 to 5 and tension between 4.19 (a visit to Corinth soon) and 16.5-9 (a delayed and lengthy trip). Or again the tension between 10.14-22 forbidding participation in temple meals, and the more open attitude in the paragraph immediately following. The result has been a variety of theories analysing 1 Corinthians into two or more letters. Others have attempted to resolve tensions by suggesting that certain passages were interpolated at a later stage (notably 11.2-16 or 14.33b-36) (fuller details can be found in Hurd, p. 45; Kümmel, pp. 275-77; and Murphy-O'Connor, 'Interpolations').

However, as Hurd and Kümmel have shown, such hypotheses are unnecessary and unsatisfactory. (1) They presuppose that everything Paul wrote to one of his churches was accorded lasting importance from the beginning. That is an unsafe assumption (cf. 2 Cor. 2.3-4; Col. 4.16). (2) It is difficult to imagine the circumstances in which different letters of Paul would have been amalgamated in quite such a scissors-and-paste manner as the various source analyses require. If it was respect for Paul which ensured the several letters' preservation it is hard to see that same respect mirrored in an editing process which certainly mangled the letters and discarded parts (not least opening and closing of the former letter) which did not fit. (3) Besides the difficulties which the partition hypotheses create for themselves, the tensions within 1 Corinthians themselves are of relatively little significance and admit various plausible historical explanations.

A recent article by Martinus de Boer, for example, argues that Paul wrote 1 Corinthians in two distinct stages: 1 Corinthians 1–4 had already been substantially drafted in response to the information brought by Chloe's people before the Stephanas group arrived with new information, which caused Paul to append chs. 5–16 to make the complete letter we now possess. This would help explain the slightly awkward jumps between chs. 4 and 5 (as also between chs. 6 and 7). Indeed, even the recognition that the letter may well have been composed over a few days, with breaks in dictation and different points nuanced to take account of different sensitivities, would be sufficient to explain such awkward transitions and tensions as are present in the letter. One might be forgiven for wondering if those who find such awkwardnesses a sign of multiple composition themselves write with the completeness of coherence and continuity which they look for in Paul.

The Art of Letter-Writing and of Rhetoric

During the last twenty years a new dimension has been brought to these older discussions of literary form by intensive studies of ancient letter-writing and rhetoric.

Students now have readily available plenty of examples of different kinds of letters written in the ancient world (see Stowers). These have confirmed the earlier conclusion drawn from the study of papyri letters at the beginning of the century: that Paul's letters would have been readily recognized as real letters, but that their length and content mark them out as distinctive within the broader genre. The most obvious similarities come in the letter's opening and closing. Hence there is a characteristic opening to a Pauline letter, with its distinctive Christian embellishments—address (typically 'to the saints'), greeting ('grace and peace'), thanksgiving ('I thank God') and prayer (all but the last featuring in 1 Corinthians). Similarly there is a typical closing—travel plans, greetings, autograph and final benediction—all of which feature in 1 Corinthians (see Weima). In addition, however, it is now also clear that throughout the body of his letters Paul made use of what may be characterized as conventional literary formulae (see further Doty). All this has made it easier to recognize 1 Corinthians not only as a real letter but also as a coherent letter.

Analysis of epistolary structure, however, has shed only so much light on the Pauline letter, mostly on the opening and closing and not much on the letter body. More fruitful has been the closely related study of Paul's letters in the light of ancient rhetoric, the art of persuasion by skilful presentation, which was such an important feature of Greco-Roman education and public life. Here the impact of Dieter Betz's ground-breaking commentary on Galatians has been considerable and has introduced students of Paul's letters to the features of classical rhetoric: *exordium* (introduction); *narratio* (narration), basic statement of the facts; *propositio* (proposition), central issues to be proved; *probatio* (confirmation), the main arguments; *refutatio* (refutation), rebuttal of opposition arguments; *peroratio* (conclusion), summary of the case (with a view to evoking a sympathetic response).

The compactness of individual sections of 1 Corinthians invite rhetorical analysis along these lines (most recently Smit on chs. 12–14 and Watson on ch. 15). But the most thoroughgoing attempt to read 1 Corinthians as a whole in the light of rhetorical forms and technique has been that of Margaret Mitchell. She sees the letter primarily as an appeal for unity, seeking to persuade the Corinthians to end their factionalism and to be reconciled to each other. In formal terms the letter is an example of deliberative rhetoric, in which the appeal is presented as for the readers' advantage and proofs are adduced by way of example. Throughout the body of the letter she finds regular use of terms and phrases appropriate to an ancient discussion of factionalism and concord (summarized on pp. 180-81).

Thus looking at the letter as a whole (and following her outline in Betz and Mitchell) we have

1.4-9	*exordium*, preceded by the letter opening (1.1-3);
1.10-17	*narratio*, beginning with 1.10, the thesis statement of the argument of the entire letter: 'I appeal to you, brothers...that all of you be in agreement and that there be no divisions among you, but that you be united in the same mind and the same purpose';
1.18–15.57	*probatio* (in four sections)
1.18–4.21	first proof, in which Paul lays the groundwork for the rest of the argument, by redefining the goals and standards by which the Christian should make decisions, by demonstrating the Corinthians' need for his advice in regard to unity by censuring them, and by arguing that he is the best one to advise them by describing his own apostolic office and responsibility (4.16);

5.1–11.1	second proof, in which Paul deals with the specific issues now dividing the community, particularly in regard to their wider relationships in Corinth;
11.2–14.40	third proof, in which Paul deals with the Corinthian divisiveness in their worship;
15.1-57	fourth proof, in which Paul deals with the divisiveness over the resurrection from the dead, the eschatological focus highlighting the final goal in relation to which the Corinthians should make their decisions;
15.58	*peroratio*, followed by the letter closing (16.1-24).

Mitchell's overall argument makes an impressive case for the letter's unity and gives a very plausible explanation of the tensions which have given rise to so many partition theories. In the event it is easy to understand the oscillations in Paul's presentation as indicative of his attempts to conciliate different groups and viewpoints. More than in any other approach to the letter we are given the sense of a living dialogue, in which Paul bent his argument in different directions and gave it different nuances in order to render his appeal more effective to different interests and individuals.

Mitchell's work allows a natural transition to the first main section of the letter, for it becomes clear from her study that the question of the *letter's* unity is in large part a reflection of the *disunity* of the church in Corinth addressed in this letter. And that disunity becomes immediately clear in 1.12 and underlies the main thrust of the first section (1.10–4.21). It is in this section, too, that Paul's own evaluation of rhetoric comes most to the fore. So it is to this section that we now turn.

For Further Reading

H.D. Betz, *Galatians* (Hermeneia; Philadelphia: Fortress Press, 1979).

H.D. Betz and M.M. Mitchell, 'Corinthians, First Epistle to the', in *Anchor Bible Dictionary* (ed. D.N. Freedman; Garden City, NY: Doubleday, 1992), I, pp. 1139-48.

B. Blue, 'Acts and the House Church', in D.W.J. Gill and C. Gempf (eds.), *The Book of Acts in its First Century Setting*. II. *Graeco-Roman Setting* (Grand Rapids: Eerdmans/Carlisle: Paternoster, 1994), pp. 119-222.

M.C. de Boer, 'The Composition of 1 Corinthians', *NTS* 40 (1994), pp. 229-45.

W.G. Doty, *Letters in Primitive Christianity* (Philadelphia: Fortress Press, 1973).

J.W. Drane, *Paul, Libertine or Legalist?* (London: SPCK, 1975).

D.W.J. Gill, 'The Meat-Market at Corinth (1 Corinthians 10.25)', *TynBul*
43.2 (1992), pp. 389-93.

J.C. Hurd, *The Origin of 1 Corinthans* (London: SPCK, 1965).

R. Jewett, *Dating Paul's Life* (London: SCM Press, 1979).

W.G. Kümmel, *Introduction to the New Testament* (London: SCM Press,
1975).

M.M. Mitchell, *Paul and the Rhetoric of Reconciliation. An Exegetical
Investigation of the Language and Composition of 1 Corinthians*
(Tübingen: Mohr/Louisville: Westminster Press, 1992).

J. Murphy-O'Connor, 'Interpolations in 1 Corinthians', *CBQ* 48 (1986),
pp. 81-94.

—*St. Paul's Corinth. Texts and Archaeology* (Collegeville, MN: Liturgical
Press, 1983).

—'Corinth', *Anchor Dictionary of the Bible*, I, pp. 1134-39.

J. Smit, 'Argument and Genre of 1 Corinthians 12-14', in S.E. Porter and
T.H. Olbricht (eds.), *Rhetoric and the New Testament: Essays from the
1992 Heidelberg Conference* (Sheffield: JSOT Press, 1993), pp. 211-30.

S.K. Stowers, *Letter Writing in Greco-Roman Antiquity* (Philadelphia:
Westminster Press, 1986).

D.F. Watson, 'Paul's Rhetorical Strategy in 1 Corinthains 15', in Porter and
Olbricht (eds.), *Rhetoric and the New Testament*, pp. 231-49.

J.A.D. Weima, *Neglected Endings: The Significance of the Pauline Letter
Closings* (JSNTSup, 101; Sheffield: JSOT Press, 1994).

3

DIVISIONS IN THE CORINTHIAN CHURCH:
1 CORINTHIANS 1–4

THE LONGEST RUNNING critical question regarding 1 Corinthians during the modern period has been the significance of the slogans in 1.12: 'Each of you says, "I belong to Paul", or "I belong to Apollos", or "I belong to Cephas", or "I belong to Christ"' The slogans appear to be linked to the talk of 'divisions' (literally 'schisms') in 1.10. And though 1.10 does not actually say that there were divisions in the Corinthian church, the other reference to 'schisms' certainly does—'I hear that there are divisions among you' (11.18). When we add in further allusions to 'quarrels' (1.11), 'jealousy and quarreling' (3.3), 'these arrogant people' (4.19), 'boasting' (5.6), 'grievances' and legal proceedings between members (6.1), 'factions' (11.19) and 'disorder' (14.33), it is hard to avoid the conclusion that the Corinthian church was riven with disagreement. In the light of this evidence a plausible deduction to be drawn is that the slogans of 1.12 are the rallying cries of four different parties.

This data has provided the agenda for a debate which has run with little check for over a century and a half. Was the letter intended to engage combatively on several different fronts? How many parties were there in Corinth? Who were they? To what extent was there actual opposition to Paul? What was its nature? Is the problem that of particular factions or of factionalism? Any illumination on these issues would certainly take the lid off earliest Christianity in a challenging (for some possibly threatening) way.

Four Parties?

On first sight, the most straightforward deduction to be drawn from 1.12 is that there were four parties or rival factions in the Corinthian church—a Paul party, an Apollos party, a Cephas party, and a Christ party—perhaps related to the different house churches in Corinth. Identifying and describing these parties, however, has been more problematic.

The least difficult to identify has been the first—the Paul party. The implication of 1.12 is that in the face of other slogans a group of Paul sympathizers had coined their own party slogan, 'I belong to Paul'. The rebuke of this attitude in 1.13-15 is still more illuminating: 'Were you baptized in the name of Paul? I thank God that I baptized none of you except Crispus and Gaius, so that no one can say that you were baptized in my name'. The clear implication is that party affiliation was being determined by reference to who had baptized whom. It was on the basis of their having been baptized by Paul that some were claiming, 'I belong to Paul'. So much so, that Paul was relieved in retrospect that he had personally baptized so few!

This allows the further inference, either that the Paul party was relatively few in number, or that the slogan presupposed baptism by one of Paul's immediate associates (Silas or Timothy?, Acts 18.5). Such questions must always bear in mind the likelihood noted in Chapter One, that the Corinthian congregation was itself relatively small (no more than about 40?).

We are also in a position to identify the Paul partisans. Presumably because they were his sympathizers they receive favourable mention in the letter—Crispus (1.14; Acts 18.8) and Gaius (1.14; Rom. 16.23); Stephanas (1.16; 16.15), and so also the other two mentioned with him, Fortunatus and Achaicus, who brought Paul the news of what was happening in Corinth (16.17); and presumably the other group reporting to Paul, Chloe's people (1.11). Were they Paul's only supporters (as few as seven or eight?), or only the most important?

In the 19th century the second most definitive of the slogans was in effect that of the Cephas party. This was because of the continuing influence of Ferdinand Christian Baur, for whom the evidence of a Pauline and Petrine faction in Corinth was the basis from which grew his whole reconstruction of early Christian history, as a long running conflict between Pauline and Petrine Christianity. In fact the debate was primarily focused on the fourth of the slogans ('I belong to Christ'), but Baur had assumed that the Christ party and the Cephas party were one and the same, Jewish Christians who claimed that their relationship with Christ came through Christ's chief apostle, Peter.

Whether Peter himself ever visited Corinth personally is far from certain; 9.5 is hardly clear cut evidence. But persuasive cases have been made by leading commentators like Johannes Weiss, T.W. Manson and C.K. Barrett, 'Cephas'. A further plausible allusion has been claimed in 3.10 ('someone else is building on' the foundation laid by Paul), since the sequence 3.5-9 (referring to Apollos), 3.10-15 (referring to Cephas?) is matched by the Paul, Apollos, Cephas sequence in 3.22. Barrett also draws particular attention to 15.11, 'Whether it was I or they, so we proclaim and so you have come to believe', where the 'they/we' can naturally be taken to include the first and last named witnesses of Christ's resurrection just mentioned (15.5, 8). If the evidence of 2 Corinthians can also be drawn in, Barrett would include other potential allusions in 2.17; 3.1; 5.12; 10.7, 12-18 and 11.4-5, 13. Thus wherever a Jewish dimension to one of the Corinthian church's problem is detectable (as in 1 Cor. 8–10 and 2 Cor. 11) it can be linked to either the influence of Cephas himself or to the presence of a Peter party in the church, consisting primarily of Christian Jews, fruit of Cephas's mission to 'the circumcision' (Gal. 2.9), and baptized either by Cephas himself or by one of his close associates.

Next to the Paul party the most obvious other faction to be deduced from the slogans of 1.12 is the Apollos party. The same two slogans are repeated in 3.4: 'one says, "I belong to Paul", and another, "I belong to Apollos" '. And the following paragraph (3.5-9) seems to be addressed to the partisans of each group: 'What then is Apollos? What is Paul?' Similarly in 4.6 Paul notes, 'I have applied all this to Apollos and myself for your benefit'. The degree to which Apollos comes back into close focus at the end of the first section (chs. 1–4) has long suggested that the first section as a whole is directed primarily against an Apollos faction.

The attractiveness of this latter hypothesis is enhanced when we recall that, according to Acts 18.24 and 28, Apollos was from Alexandria and was an eloquent and powerful expositor of the Scriptures. For the Jewish community in Alexandria was famed for its wisdom literature and Paul's elder contemporary, Philo of Alexandria, for his allegorical expositions of the Scriptures. It is an easy step of the historical imagination, therefore, to identify those rebuked consistently throughout 1.17–3.23 for their false evaluation of wisdom and clever speech with Apollos or with an Apollos faction. These would be the Apollos party, including some of Paul's own converts won over by Apollos's impressive rhetoric (cf. 3.6-8), as well, presumably, as others converted by Apollos himself (cf. 1.13-15).

The most controversial of the four parties inferred from the slogans of 1.12, however, has been the Christ party. The problem is that the Christ party is even more ephemeral than the Cephas party. Cephas is at least referred to in an argumentative way elsewhere (3.22 and 9.5), but the only other plausible allusion to a Christ slogan as such is 2 Cor. 10.7: 'If you are confident that you belong to Christ, remind yourself of this, that just as you belong to Christ, so also do we'. That does not sound like a rebuke to a faction who claimed some sort of exclusive belonging to Christ. And the absence of 'Christ' from 3.22 ('whether Paul or Apollos or Cephas') weakens the argument that 'I am of Christ' is a party slogan quite like the others.

Baur had resolved the problem of lack of direct information about the Christ party by his assumption that the last slogan, 'I belong to Christ', was a slogan used by the Peter party. Long before, Chrysostom and other church fathers took the 'I belong to Christ' as Paul's own personal confession. That, however, would have required a clearer indication that the fourth slogan was to be read more as a rejoinder to the other three. Whereas the much more obvious reading of 1.13a, 'Has Christ been divided?', is as itself a rebuke to the immediately preceding slogan. Weiss had attempted to

resolve the issue by taking the final slogan, 'I belong to
Christ', as a marginal annotation (it is omitted in the allusion to 1.12 in *1 Clem.* 47.3), perhaps a protest from some
pious reader disgusted at such factional talk, which had then
been incorporated into the text by subsequent scribes. But
that too makes hard work of the immediately following question: what prompted Paul to ask, 'Has Christ been divided?',
if not the slogan, 'I belong to Christ'; and if the question was
already in the text, would that not have discouraged the
pious glossator and scribe from inserting the slogan before it?

In twentieth century discussion, however, the issue of a
Christ party has been caught up in the history of religions
attempt to identify the opposition to Paul in Corinth as
Gnostics. And that requires a separate discussion.

No Parties?

The difficulty of identifying four parties in the Corinthian
church has encouraged many scholars to look for a simpler
solution. Baur had envisaged only two parties, but had
achieved that solution by amalgamating the evidence regarding the Paul and Apollos slogans over against that relating to
the Cephas and Christ slogans. That is, he lumped together
the two strongest sets of evidence and the two weakest sets
of evidence, so that the case for his second party (the Christ-
Cephas party) was exceedingly thin.

It is true that 1.13 might seem to set 'Christ' and 'Paul' in
some degree of antithesis: 'Has Christ been divided? Was
Paul crucified for you? Or were you baptized in the name of
Paul?' But Weiss effectively destroyed that case: (1) the question ('Has Christ been divided?') does not actually meet the
case where one faction is making exclusive claim to Christ
(they would respond, 'No, he is wholly ours'); (2) the next two
questions ('Was Paul crucified for you? Were you baptized in
the name of Paul?') similarly invite a response ('No: Christ
was; in the name of Christ') which would play into the hands
of those making exclusive claim to Christ; (3) the conclusion
of 3.23, 'you belong to Christ', would again play into the
hands of a Christ party; and (4) 3.21, 'let no one boast about
human leaders', would be a singularly inapposite rebuke if

the Corinthian opposition included a Christ party.

Of the other two hypothesized parties, only an Apollos party seemed to be given much substance from the text itself (particularly 3.3-4). In this case the problem is that Paul speaks so positively of Apollos; there is no sense of tension between the two in Paul's description of their work as mutually and cooperatively fruitful (3.5-9). And in 16.12 it appears to be the Corinthians (in their letter) who have asked Paul concerning Apollos. Had there been an Apollos faction as such, we would have expected the communication to be quite different. Either the Apollos partisans had direct access to Apollos himself; in which case the church could have found out Apollos's plans without asking Paul. Or Paul in his letter, in the light of his good relations with Apollos, would have been able to call on him to rebuke the faction which looked to Apollos as their leader. As for the 'Paul party' itself, it is perhaps sufficient to note that Paul is more critical of the 'I belong to Paul' slogan than of any other (1.13). He does not side with one 'party' against the rest; he criticizes party spirit however manifested.

The difficulties in reading the 1.12 slogans as evidence of two or more parties as such have caused others to seek for alternative solutions. The most sharply contrasting has been that of Johannes Munck. As part of a larger reaction against the Baur thesis of earliest Christian history as dominated by the opposition between Petrine and Pauline Christianity, Munck disputed entirely the hypothesis of a Jewish Christian opposition to Paul in Corinth. In his view the evidence does not point to the presence of factions at all, but only to 'cliques'. Nor does it indicate that Paul was confronted by any coherent theological positions on matters of doctrine or practice, but only 'bickerings'. Most striking of all is the fact that Paul does not address individuals or factions, but speaks to the church as a whole—and not least in 1.12-13.

Munck probably went too far in his reaction to Baur. It seems hard to doubt that Paul was confronted by some sharp criticism if not outright opposition from within the church in Corinth. We need only think of the sharpness of his response in passages like 1.17; 3.1-3; 4.18-21; 8.1-3 and 11.16. Two are particularly worth noting: 4.3, 'With me it is a very small thing that I should be judged by you or by any human court'; and 9.3, 'This is my defence to those who would examine me'. Paul would be expressing himself very oddly in these passages if he was not well aware that he had come under criticism from within the Corinthian assembly. It is not necessary to draw in the further evidence of 2 Cor. 3.1 and chs. 10–13, since the sharper antagonism evident in that letter could be the result of further developments and new arrivals in Corinth subsequent to 1 Corinthians. A solution which takes more account of these factors is that of Nils Dahl. He argues that 1.10–4.21 is best characterized as an apology for Paul's apostolic ministry, and that the quarrels in the Corinthian church were mainly due to a substantial opposition against Paul in the church established by him. The solution to the puzzle of 1.12 is then simple.

> Those who said 'I belong to Paul' were proud of him and held that his excellence surpassed that of Apollos or Cephas. The other slogans are all to be understood as declarations of independence from Paul. Apollos is mentioned as the most outstanding Christian teacher who had visited Corinth after Paul. Cephas is the famous pillar, the first witness to the resurrection, an apostle before Paul. The slogan 'I belong to Christ' is not the motto of a specific 'Christ-party' but simply means 'I belong myself to Christ—and am independent of Paul' (Dahl, p. 322).

Even so, however, it is unclear whether Dahl takes sufficient account of 4.18-19, 'But some of you, thinking that I am not coming to you, have become arrogant. But I will come to you soon, if the Lord wills, and I will find out not the talk of these arrogant people, but their power'. This seems to indicate that Paul had in mind a particular group, and not just a generalized opposition. Or perhaps we should better say, particular individuals. Moreover, the talk of 'power' introduces a fresh dimension to the debate which will require further analysis in the next chapter.

At all events it has already become clear that the situation confronted in 1 Corinthians is not readily amenable to an analysis simply in terms of the slogans of 1.12, or to be reduced to the confrontation of a number of clearly defined parties or factions. Some of our initial questions can therefore be given a provisional answer. But it remains unclear

whether there was general unrest, quarreling and antagonism to Paul, or rather a sequence of tensions set up by a
relatively small number of 'arrogant' individuals.

Gnosticism in Corinth?

If 1.12 has provided one focus for discussion about the situation confronting Paul in Corinth, the other main focus has
been provided by what can fairly be regarded as the principal
word of the section—*sophia* (wisdom). Discussion over the
past century has fluctuated among three major hypotheses:
attempts to explain the language and themes (particularly of
chs. 1–4) in terms either of Gnosticism, or of Hellenistic-
Judaism, or of rhetoric. The fluctuations in debate regarding
these three options reflect the broader course of developments in New Testament studies during this period.

During the middle decades of the twentieth century discussion was dominated by the attempt to find a unified opposition to Paul in Gnosticism. This was principally a spin-off of
the history of religions research of the first half of the
century, notably that of Rudolf Bultmann. From this had
emerged the strongly promoted conclusion that Gnosticism
could no longer be seen simply as a second-century Christian
heresy. There was already at the time of Christianity a form
of Gnosticism, indeed a pre-Christian Gnosis, which probably
influenced the development of Christian thought and
praxis. The discovery of the Nag Hammadi texts in the late
1940s gave the hypothesis a shot in the arm, when it might
otherwise have faded away.

In this search for early Gnosticism 1 Corinthians once
again provided prime evidence. There were evidently those
in the Corinthian church who regarded themselves as
'pneumatics' (*pneumatikoi*) (particularly 3.1)—a key term of
identification in later Gnostic systems. This would help
explain the attitude to the sacraments which Paul seems to
contest in chs. 1 and 10 (so e.g. Painter, p. 245). That is,
baptism as effecting a spiritual bond between the baptizand
and the baptizer, the latter perhaps understood as a kind of
mystagogue, leading the former into the mysteries of the new
cult (hence 1.14-17). And the Lord's Supper as spiritual

(pneumatic) food, that is, conveying the Spirit to the partaker and guaranteeing spiritual blessing thereafter (hence the warning of 10.5-12). It would also explain the Corinthians' concern regarding 'pneumatics' (either spiritual things or spiritual persons) in the questions they seem to have put to Paul in their letter (12.1).

Other evidence readily understood as supporting the Gnostic hypothesis were the prominence of two further typically Gnostic terms: 'knowledge' (*gnosis*) and 'wisdom' (*sophia*). The former gave ready explanation of the problem confronted in ch. 8, where the term occurs five times in eleven verses. The problem being that certain Corinthian Christians, confident of their superior knowledge (idols do not really exist, 8.4), felt no qualms in eating meat which had been sacrificed to idols. This could imply a group of Corinthian Gnostics who rejoiced in their own liberty and looked down on other Christians who had not yet attained to this higher insight into reality. The emphasis on 'wisdom' throughout the first three chapters (16 times) gives the same impression, since evidently Paul was confronting a pride in wisdom which devalued others who lacked this wisdom (1.18–2.5; 3.19). Similarly the realized eschatology of 4.8 ('Already you have all you want! Already you have become rich!') could be said to tie in neatly with 15.12 ('some of you say there is no resurrection of the dead') in a Gnostic-like claim that the resurrection was already past (cf. 2 Tim. 2.18).

Early on in the century such issues were brought to the fore by Richard Reitzenstein who opened up the subject in a famous treatment of 'Paul as Pneumatic' (1927), in which he observed that Paul himself speaks in 1 Corinthians as a gnostic (2.6-16). But it was Walter Schmithals in his 1954 dissertation under Bultmann at Marburg, who brought the Gnostic thesis to full expression. Schmithals argued that in both Corinthian epistles Paul faced a single front—Jewish Gnosticism—and that all features of this Corinthian theology came under the overarching concept of 'Gnosis'. In particular, the discussion of chs. 6–15 was either occasioned by the Gnostics (7.40), or focused on the problems occasioned by Gnostic libertinism and disparagement of the flesh.

Less clear was the scope of the Corinthian Gnostics'

Christology. One of Schmithals's most striking claims is that in 12.3 the utterance 'Let Jesus be cursed' was an expression of the Gnostics' Christology, separating the man Jesus from the heavenly being Christ and treating the former with disdain (he had been anticipated by Wilhelm Lütgert in 1908). On the other hand, Schmithals had denied that the Corinthian Gnostics knew Christ as a heavenly redeemer figure. Only a few years later, however, Ulrich Wilckens capped Schmithals by arguing that in the background of 2.6-8 lay the Gnostic idea of the descent of the heavenly Redeemer through the realms of the archons, influential already in Corinth in an early form of the Jewish Gnostic Sophia myth (cf. *1 Enoch* 42).

Wilckens's contribution was the high-water mark of the Gnostic hypothesis in reference to 1 Corinthians. But since then it has been in steady retreat. Partly it has been a question of terminology. A consensus was reached at the Messina Colloquium on the Origins of Gnosticism in 1966 that the term Gnosticism (or Gnosis) should be restricted to the Gnostic systems which first emerged in the second century, and that 'gnosis' or 'proto-gnosticism' should be used for the earlier period. With this distinction in mind it was reasonable still to speak of Corinthian 'gnosis' or 'proto-gnosticism', on the grounds that some (at least) of the Corinthians evidently expressed attitudes and acted on beliefs which were subsequently to feature prominently in the later Gnostic systems (hence also Dunn, *Unity*, pp. 277-79; Wilson, 'Gnosis').

On the other hand, the continued use of the term 'gnosticism' (or 'Gnosticism') with reference to the Corinthian church may simply be anachronistic and misleading. The distinctive features of these later systems are not evident in the first-century period: the hunt for a pre-Christian Gnostic or Primal Man Redeemer myth has been a wild goose chase; and there is nothing in the New Testament period of the degree of antipathy between spirit and matter ('flesh' as a substance) so fundamental to the later Gnosticisms. As Robin Wilson, the principal British contributor to the debate comments:

All too often a 'pre-Christian gnosis' is postulated on the basis of
the evidence we have, then to provide firmer contours and give it
substance the main features of second-century Gnosticism are
projected into the first century, and we end with the hypothetical
influence upon Paul and early Christianity of a 'pre-Christian
Gnosticism' for which there is no real evidence and which results
from reading first-century documents with second-century specta-
cles ('Gnosis', p. 109).

Not only so, but the other terms so characteristic of the
Corinthian divisions, including 'gnosis' and 'sophia', were a
matter of widespread aspiration in the Mediterranean world
and not the property of any one philosophy or system.
Understandably, therefore, the 1960s and 70s witnessed
several attempts to explain the situation in Corinth without
recourse to the Gnostic hypothesis.

Hellenistic Judaism Wisdom and/or Spiritual Enthusiasm?

The search for pre-Christian Gnosticism had naturally made
great play with the figure (or myth) of Jewish Wisdom,
particularly as found in a passage like ben Sira 24 and in the
Jewish Alexandrian philosopher Philo. But once that range
of material had been disentangled from the quest for a pre-
Christian Gnostic Redeemer myth it could prove renewedly
fruitful for illuminating the background of 1 Corinthians 1–4.

Notable here has been Richard Horsley's refinement of an
earlier thesis by Birger Pearson. Like Reitzenstein before
them, Pearson and Horsley ('Pneumatikos') focused on the
term *pneumatikos*, particularly in its antithesis with
psychikos (2.13–3.1), but in this case against the background
of Philo's interpretation of Gen. 2.7. For although Hellenistic
Judaism does not use that specific terminology, the contrast
could reflect Philo's distinction between two types of human
beings, the earthly man of Gen. 2.7a and the heavenly man
of Gen. 2.7b, and so the adjectives describe two classes of
persons or two levels of spirituality. This is the clue for
Horsley: the terms in 1 Corinthians 2–3 probably denote
different levels of spiritual experience, status or achieve-
ment. The contrasts in the same context, 'mature/infant'
(*teleios/nepios*, 2.6/3.1) and 'wise/foolish' (*sophos/moros*, 1.25-

27), also reflect the Jewish Wisdom tradition and point to the same conclusion. James Davis has pushed Horsley's thesis still further, by pointing out the strong link between Wisdom and Spirit in the Jewish Wisdom tradition, a feature which may well have increased the appeal of this wisdom to Corinthian spirituality. He also notes the link between wisdom and Torah in Jewish thought and hypothesizes a stronger Torah element in the Corinthian 'mix' than is clearly evident.

Here in its central elements is a hypothesis which goes a long way to explaining what Paul had in view in 2.6–3.4—a hungering for and claim to a deeper spirituality (wisdom)—giving clearer insight into God's secret wisdom. Paul did not dispute the desirability of such wisdom, indeed he claimed it for himself, but the way the Corinthians were going about it, with their jealousy and quarreling, was for him the very antithesis of that wisdom. And so far as the Christology of 1 Corinthians 1–2 is concerned, the influence is best under-stood as directly from Jewish reflection on the figure of divine wisdom rather than via a gnostic adaptation of Jewish Wisdom (so already Wilson, 'Gnostic', pp. 72-74).

If Gnosticism is an unnecessary hypothesis to explain the features and tensions of the Corinthian church as reflected in 1 Corinthians 1–3, the same is equally true of the rest of the letter. Already before Schmithals, Lütgert had suggested as an alternative to Gnostics that the opponents of Paul were 'libertine pneumatics'; and more recently Gordon Fee traces the problem to the Corinthians' assumption that they are *pneumatikoi* (presumably by reason of their experience of the Spirit) while not being so sure about Paul. Certainly the 'already' emphasis of 4.8 need only imply a spiritual enthu-siasm which gloried so much in what had already been granted (cf. 1.4-7) that it assumed that salvation was already theirs. Hence also the warning of 10.1-12. Similarly chs. 8–10 expresses a confidence in spiritual liberty and maturity which certainly uses 'gnosis' (knowledge) as a catchword, but which hardly needs to presuppose a distinctively gnostic/ Gnostic motif to make complete sense of the text.

The intervening chapters (5–7) pose the biggest problem to the pan-Gnostic hypothesis. It can provide no reason (from

Gnosis) to explain why one member of the church in Corinth was taking another to court (1 Cor. 6). On the other hand, it could provide an explanation of each of the other two main issues dealt with in these chapters. The licentiousness of the conduct indicted in chs. 5 and 6 makes some sense on the assumption of Gnostic license and liberty: since the material body counts for nothing it could be sated and indulged without effect on the spirit. Likewise the asceticism reflected in ch. 7 could make sense against a Gnostic background: since the material body counts for nothing it should be dealt with harshly and should not be indulged. The problem comes when we try to hold both explanations together. That there was a group of Gnostics or proto-gnostics who formed a united front against Paul on all other points dealt with in the letter but who radically parted company with each other on the issue of license or asceticism in conduct puts a strain on the historical imagination, not forgetting the likely size of the church as a whole. That both practices featured in Corinth seems clear; credibility only becomes strained when both practices are attributed to the same group and on the basis of the same philosophy.

The most striking element in the Gnostic hypothesis—that 12.3 ('accursed be Jesus') was a Corinthian Gnostic slogan—fares no better than the others. The context (12.1-11) certainly seems to envisage a cry uttered in the context of worship, thus ruling out an otherwise attractive suggestion that renunciation of Christ under trial or torture was in view. But there is no indication elsewhere in the Corinthian correspondence that a Gnostic-like distinction between (the human) Jesus and (the heavenly) Christ was anywhere in view. On the contrary, the double name 'Jesus Christ' or 'Christ Jesus' is used as freely in 1 and 2 Corinthians as elsewhere in Paul, assuredly indicating no sense of tension at that point. The hypothesis also requires a congregation who were so heavily influenced by this advanced Gnostic Christology that such an outburst during the assembly's worship could be counted as acceptable. Much more plausible is the alternative suggestion that the issue had arisen as a question by the Corinthians because of an incident in which someone speaking apparently under inspiration during the

Corinthians' charismatic worship had uttered the exclama-
tion (Dunn, *Jesus*, p. 420 n. 180). In other words, what we
have is another indication of spiritual enthusiasm in Corinth
(so also 14.12) rather than already developed Gnostic beliefs.

The only other plausible indicator of Corinthian
Gnosticism is the denial of the resurrection of the dead in
15.12. It is not that the Corinthians questioned whether
Jesus had been raised. In that case Paul's rejoinder would
have fallen on deaf ears; for Paul's reply seems to be based
on the resurrection of Christ as the agreed starting point
(15.12). What seems rather to have been at issue was
whether there was still a future resurrection to be awaited
by believers. And the chief problem seems to have been the
Corinthians' difficulty in envisaging *how* it could happen,
what kind of body would be involved (15.35).

There may, therefore, be something of the Greek disparagement of the physical here, an incredulity that the material body could be saved. But the terms Paul uses in his
response make it unlikely that a sharper Gnostic antithesis
between flesh and Spirit is in view. For though he denies
that 'flesh and blood' can inherit the kingdom (15.50), his
comparison between the diversity of different kinds of
flesh and the diversity of different kinds of body in 15.38-40
would have been misleading in an anti-gnostic polemic. It
makes better sense to see his distinction between the
'natural (physical) body' of this life and the 'spiritual body' of
the resurrection (15.44) as an attempt to re-express Jewish
understanding of existence as always an embodied existence
in a way which made more sense to those who thought in
Greek terms. Here too, then, it would make greater sense of
the text to follow Anthony Thiselton (or Horsley's 'Spiritual
Elitism') in assuming that the problem addressed in ch. 15
was again that of overenthusiasm finding it hard to concep-
tualize what (if anything) was still outstanding in the
process of salvation.

In short, the Gnostic hypothesis as an explanation for the
divisions in the Corinthian church has proved itself to be
increasingly unsatisfactory as the century has progressed,
particularly as the hypothesis of a united opposition to Paul.
Most of the data is much more amenable to the hypothesis of

an influence from Hellenistic Judaism and/or pneumatic enthusiasm. However, we have still to look at the third hypothesis used to shed light on chs. 1–4 in particular.

Rhetoric and Politics

The discussion so far has not adequately reflected the full range of Paul's talk of 'wisdom' in the opening chapters of 1 Corinthians. For there are two negative kinds of wisdom combatted by Paul. One is 'the wisdom of the world' (1.20), 'human wisdom' (1.25; 2.13), the 'wisdom of this age' (2.6). This clearly stands in antithesis to the 'wisdom from above' so central to the Jewish Wisdom tradition. Both Paul and the Corinthians laid claim to that wisdom, though Paul disputed the latters' claim because of the divisiveness which it had generated in the Corinthian assemblies. This is the 'wisdom' which has dominated the discussion so far reviewed.

However, as Barrett ('Christianity') observed in reference to Wilckens, *sophia* is also used by Paul in a negative way to denote a kind of eloquence, a technique of persuasion (1.17, 19-20; 2.1, 4-5, 13). In point of fact, Paul does not attribute 'the wisdom of the world' to his Corinthian critics. But he does imply that they were making too much of the wisdom of human speech (2.1-5) and were thus in serious danger of mistaking the character of divine wisdom (now recognized by its focus in Christ crucified) and the way it came to effect ('in demonstration of the Spirit and of power'). This overevaluation of human rhetoric, linked with their jealousy and quarreling, in effect put them back on the level of human wisdom (3.1-4).

This rhetorical dimension to the issues in 1 Corinthians 1–3 had been recognized at the beginning of the century (again particularly by Weiss), but had been largely lost to sight for two reasons: partly because rhetoric itself was understood too narrowly and negatively as concern with mere form, a cultivating of expression at the expense of content, concern merely with ornamentation; and partly because the rhetorical features were ignored during the ascendancy of the Gnostic hypothesis. Here too Horsley ('Wisdom') had demonstrated how much *sophia* as persuasive speech could be illuminated against the background of Hellenistic-Jewish tradition represented by Philo and the Wisdom of Solomon. Now, however, the more recent move to read Paul's letters in the light of rhetorical conventions of the time has brought fresh light to the whole passage.

Indicative of this revival of interest in rhetoric as the key to interpreting 1 Corinthians 1–3 is the recent work of Duane Litfin, who has pointed out that the most common context in which the average first-century citizen of the Greco-Roman world used the term *sophia* would be rhetoric. Moroever it can be confidently assumed that the practice of rhetoric was held in highest esteem in the educated circles of a city like Corinth. He cites the cautionary word of Eduard Norden, the doyen of study in this area, that 'we will simply fail to grasp the import of 1 Cor. 1.17–2.5 unless we remember that Paul wrote these words at a time when it was not possible to be considered wise without being eloquent' (Litfin, p. 244). It is this background which, for Litfin, gives the most satisfying answers to the interpretative questions of 1 Corinthians 1–4 and precludes the need to look for others; 'the rhetorical interpretation makes complete sense of the entire section' (Litfin, p. 10). In this light it can be seen that Paul's goal is to defend his *modus operandi* as a preacher over against the appeal of rhetoric classically conceived. Paul, we may say, sets the *sophia* of the cross against the *sophia* of rhetoric, theological rhetoric over against the rhetoric of eloquence.

Litfin has seen chs. 1–4 as a clash of rhetoric. But an earlier study by L.L. Welborn had already demonstrated an inescapable social and political dimension to the situation addressed in chs. 1–4. He noted that the terms used by Paul in these chapters had also been used to characterize conflicts within city-states by Greco-Roman historians: *schisma* ('schism'), *eris* ('strife'), *meris* ('party')—should 1.13 be translated, 'Has the body of Christ been split into parties?'; 'puffed up', language 'all too familiar to the student of political history as the caricature of the political windbag' (Welborn, pp. 88); *hoi teleioi* (2.6), usually taken in the sense 'mature', could also be taken in the sense 'the influential', 'those in office'; 4.1-5 indicates that Paul's opponents sought to 'examine' his credentials in quasi-judicial proceedings, a kind

of ecclesiastical court' (pp. 107-108). In such political factionalism rhetoric, precisely as the art of persuasion, obviously
also played a part. From this he deduces that

> the real problem addressed in 1 Corinthians 1–4 is one of parti-
> sanship...it is a power struggle, not a theological controversy,
> which motivates the writing of 1 Corinthians 1–4...Paul's goal in
> 1 Corinthians 1–4 is not the refutation of heresy, but...the preven-
> tion of *stasis* (strife, discord) (pp. 89-90).

Similarly Stephen Pogoloff draws attention to the close
correlation in the ancient world between status and
eloquence: *sophia* as rhetoric implies far more than just technical skill in speaking but a whole world of social status; it is
the socially or politically powerful who have been trained in
the art of rhetoric. Hence the use of a word like *suzetetes*
('debater') in 1.20, and the progression from 1.18-25 on
through 1.26ff. What Paul objects to is the attempt to play off
Apollos and himself against each other in terms of their
rhetorical ability, seen as a measure of their social status, of
their stature as 'wise men'. Paul is not unwilling to meet
such false evaluation of rhetoric with his own rhetorical skill,
but the 'maturity' he claims is not the perfect synthesis of
wisdom and eloquence but the wisdom given by the unveiling
of the divine mystery, talk by the Spirit (2.6-16).

It is principally on Welborn's conclusions that Mitchell,
referred to in the previous chapter, has so effectively built in
her overarching thesis that the letter was not against
particular parties or siding with a particular party, but
against factionalism. In his recent review of the debate
William Baird comes to the same conclusion: Paul contends
against not a single front or clearly identifiable factions, but
against factionalism and the arrogance which has fostered it.
In using the language he chose, Paul would no doubt be
conscious of such social and political dimensions to the unity
for which he appealed.

If Litfin underplayed the socio-political dimension to the
situation addressed in 1 Corinthians 1–4, Welborn and the
others have underplayed the theological dimension. As we
noted earlier, 'wisdom' is used in several senses in these
chapters, only one of which is to be immediately identified
with rhetoric. 1 Corinthians 1–3, indeed (if we link the last

two sections together), seems to reflect an intriguing interaction between Jewish and Greek wisdom among the Corinthian Christians, where some of them assumed too readily that the two were closely related: that the wisdom which gave pneumatic status and made 'mature' would also be expressed with rhetorically pleasing effect. It was presumably this rhetorical wisdom (or the interaction) which Paul had in mind in 1.22, when he attributes desire for wisdom to 'Greeks' (rather than 'Jews'). Certainly in 2.4 it will be no accident that Paul uses the word 'demonstration' (*apodeixis*), a more or less technical term in rhetoric to denote a compelling conclusion drawn out from accepted premises. The Christ-wisdom works differently, through the Spirit and power of God, irrespective of the adequacy or otherwise of the human speaker. The maturity Paul claims is apocalyptic wisdom rather than rhetorical wisdom.

However, the contributions of Welborn, Mitchell and Pogoloff have made it clear that there is a social and indeed political dimension to the situation in Corinth, as indeed to Paul's own handling of it, and it is that dimension to which we now turn.

For Further Reading

W. Baird, ' "One Against the Other": Intra-Church Conflict in 1 Corinthians', in R. T. Fortna & B. R. Gaventa (eds.), *The Conversation Continues: Studies in Paul and John: In Honor of J.L.Martyn* (Nashville: Abingdon, 1990), pp. 116-36.

C.K. Barrett, 'Christianity at Corinth', and 'Cephas and Corinth', in *Essays on Paul* (London: SPCK, 1982), pp. 1-27 and 28-39.

F.C. Baur—see W.G. Kümmel, *The New Testament: the History of the Investigation of its Problems* (Nashville: Abingdon, 1972/London: SCM Press, 1973), pp. 127-30.

N.A. Dahl, 'Paul and the Church at Corinth according to 1 Corinthians 1-4', in W.R. Farmer *et al.* (eds.), *Christian History and Interpretation. Studies presented to John Knox* (Cambridge: Cambridge University Press, 1967), pp. 313-35.

J.A. Davis, *Wisdom and Spirit. An Investigation of 1 Corinthians 1.18–3.20 against the Background of Jewish Sapiential Traditions in the Greco-Roman Period* (Lanham, MD: University Press of America, 1984).

J.D.G. Dunn, *Jesus and the Spirit: A Study of the Religious Experience of Jesus and the First Christians as Reflected in the New Testament* (London: SCM Press/Philadelphia: Westminster Press, 1975).

—*Unity and Diversity in the New Testament* (London: SCM Press/ Philadelphia: Trinity Press International, 2nd edn, 1990).

R.A. Horsley, 'Pneumatikos vs. Psychikos: Distinctions of Spiritual Status among the Corinthians', *HTR* 69 (1976), pp. 269-88.

—'Wisdom of Word and Words of Wisdom in Corinth', *CBQ* 39 (1977), pp. 224-39.

—' "How can some of you say that there is no resurrection of the dead?": Spiritual Elitism in Corinth', *NovT* 20 (1978), pp. 203-31.

D. Litfin, *St Paul's Theology of Proclamation: 1 Corinthians 1-4 and Greco-Roman Rhetoric* (Cambridge: Cambridge University Press, 1994).

T.W. Manson, 'The Corinthian Correspondence (1)', in *Studies in the Gospels and Epistles* (Manchester: Manchester University Press, 1962), pp. 190-209.

J. Munck, 'The Church without Factions', in *Paul and the Salvation of Mankind* (London: SCM Press, 1959).

J. Painter, 'Paul and the *pneumatikoi* at Corinth', in M.D. Hooker and S.G. Wilson (eds.), *Paul and Paulinism: Essays in Honour of C. K. Barrett* (London: SPCK, 1982), pp. 237-50.

B.A. Pearson, *The Pneumatikos-Psychikos Terminology in 1 Corinthians* (SBLDS, 12; Missoula, MT: Scholars Press, 1973).

S.M. Pogoloff, *Logos and Sophia: The Rhetorical Situation of 1 Corinthians* (SBLDS, 134; Atlanta: Scholars Press, 1992).

R. Reitzenstein, *Hellenistic Mystery Religions: Their Basic Ideas and Significance* (Pittsburg: Pickwick Press, 1978).

W. Schmithals, *Gnosticism in Corinth* (Nashville: Abingdon, 1971).

A.C. Thiselton, 'Realized Eschatology at Corinth', *NTS* 24 (1977–78), pp. 510-26.

L.L. Welborn, 'On the Discord in Corinth: 1 Corinthians 1–4 and Ancient Politics', *JBL* 106 (1987), pp. 85-111.

U. Wilckens, '*sophia*', *TDNT*, VII, pp. 519-22, drawing on his earlier *Weisheit und Torheit* (Tübingen: Mohr, 1959).

R.McL. Wilson, 'How Gnostic were the Corinthians?', *NTS* 19 (1972–73), pp. 65-74.

—'Gnosis at Corinth', in Hooker and Wilson (eds.), *Paul and Paulinism* (see Painter), pp. 102-14.

4

BETWEEN CHURCH AND WORLD:
SOCIAL TENSIONS IN THE CORINTHIAN
CHURCH: 1 CORINTHIANS 6–10

The Importance of Social Status

IN THE MID-1970s a series of articles by Gerd Theissen opened a new chapter in the study of 1 Corinthians, as indeed of Pauline Christianity as a whole. The John the Baptist of this new movement had been the Australian scholar Edwin Judge, but it was only the impact of Theissen's work which opened eyes to the value of the earlier contribution (as Malherbe also indicates).

The starting point is the one already alluded to in the final section of Chapter Three, 1.26-29:

> Consider your own call, brothers and sisters: not many of you were wise by human standards, not many were powerful, not many were of noble birth. But God chose what is foolish in the world to shame the wise; God chose what is weak in the world to shame the strong; God chose what is low and despised in the world, things that are not, to reduce to nothing things that are, so that no one might boast in the presence of God.

Previously attention had focused principally on Paul's main claim: that the bulk of the Corinthian Christians (and Christians generally) were those reckoned of low rank in the social order. And from this a powerful theological apologetic (some would say rationalization) can be quickly drawn, as Paul goes on to show. But Theissen focused attention on the social facts indicated in the text themselves and began to ask whether the significance of these factors had been given sufficient recognition in explaining both the tensions confronting Paul in the Corinthian church and Paul's own handling of them (earlier Judge, 'Scholastic Community', pp. 129-31).

The text tells us at once a crucial feature of the Corinthian congregation—that it was marked by social stratification. The majority of the members came from the lower classes; but the 'not many' of 1 Cor. 1.26 does not mean 'none'. On the contrary, there were a few influential members who came from the upper classes. The 'wise' would belong to the educated classes; as already observed in the preceding chapter, a good education (not least in rhetoric) would be a privilege of the well-to-do. The 'powerful' would be influential people. The 'nobly born' speaks for itself. As Welborn (pp. 96-97; see Chapter Three above) was to point out later, these are all terms employed by Greek writers from the time of Solon (sixth-century Athenian politician) to designate major class divisions involved in political discord. For Theissen the sociological implications of the language were inescapable.

Moreover, and most important for an understanding of the internal dynamics of the Corinthian congregation, the fact that this upper class group was a minority should not be taken to imply their relative insignificance in the church. Quite the contrary, their social status was bound to be a factor in the factionalism and tensions afflicting the Corinthian church. Though a minority, their social status would give them a disproportionate influence, so that we may have to speak of a dominant minority.

Theissen proceeds to draw together what we know of this influential minority. In particular, Crispus had been ruler of the synagogue (Acts 18.8): since upkeep of a synagogue required money, the office was likely to be entrusted to a man of wealth. Erastus, as 'city treasurer' (Rom. 16.23), would have been a man of influence, and if he is indeed the Erastus who laid a pavement 'at his own expense' (Chapter 2 above p. 16), he would have been a man of private wealth. Stephanas had a household (1.16; 16.15) presumably including slaves—a sure sign of high social status and wealth. Phoebe of Cenchreae (the eastern port of Corinth)

(Rom. 16.2) was a *prostatis* (patron), a point surprisingly not
made by Theissen but noted by Meeks (p. 60), so again a
figure of power and influence. Gaius (Rom. 16.23) had a
house big enough to take the whole church. Priscilla and
Aquila (16.19) seem to have run a business, involving travel,
itself an expensive affair, and to have been able to act as
Paul's host. Chloe's people (1.11) were probably slaves or
dependent workers.

Two striking points emerge. One is that the great majority
of the Corinthians known to us by name probably enjoyed
high social status. Those of lower status hardly appear as
individuals or are not named by Paul. In all probability those
named, those of high social status, were also the most active
and important members of the congregation (Theissen,
pp. 95-96). The second is the fact that, on the above analysis,
all those baptized by Paul (1.14-16, Crispus, Stephanas and
Gaius) belonged to the upper strata of society (Theissen,
pp. 102). It is notable then that, despite 1.26-29, Paul seems
to have conformed in some degree to current social mores by
perhaps targetting certain influential figures in his own
evangelism, and by personally linking himself to them
through baptism. Likewise his commendation of the
Stephanas household and the group with Stephanas in
16.15-18 is not simply Paul's attempt to reinforce a faction
identified with him, but his public alliance with one group
whose influence in the church and wider community would
be at least partly a function of Stephanas's social status.

I have so far dealt with only one of Theissen's essays, and
will have to refer to him in subsequent sections of this chapter, but it is perhaps appropriate at this point to pause and
highlight the importance of his contributions, for the
influence of his work has been phenomenal. Where previously analysis of the Corinthian situation had been almost
wholly determined by theological and religious factors,
Theissen, and the recognition his work achieved, made it
impossible to ignore social factors. Theissen showed how
much previous commentary on 1 Corinthians had been a
form of theological reductionism, attempts to explicate what
were evidently much more socially complex interactions in
too purely and isolatedly religious terms. In 1 Corinthians

more than anywhere else the theological and religious factors are thoroughly intertwined with the social, the theology thoroughly socialized, both the questions posed to Paul and Paul's own answers framed with a view to social realities. To be sure, Theissen is vulnerable to the criticism that he pushed the pendulum too far in the other direction and countered theological reductionism with a sociological reductionism (all the problems of the Corinthian church resulting from class conflict); but perhaps that was necessary if the sociological perspective was to be given the attention it clearly deserved.

The most important single contribution to emerge from the sociological approach pioneered by Theissen has been the large monograph by Wayne Meeks. This is a much broader study dealing with the wide range of social factors which must have played some part in the shaping of the Pauline churches and in Paul's dealings with them, and again we will have to refer further to Meeks when looking at some of the particular issues treated by Paul in 1 Corinthians. For the moment, however, we need simply note the elaboration and critique which Meeks has made of Theissen's basic analysis of social stratification in the Corinthian church. The main elaboration is his observation that the typical Pauline congregation reflected a fair cross-section of urban society, but with the extreme top and bottom of the Greco-Roman social scale missing from the picture (Meeks, p. 73). The main critique is that Theissen assumed that high status entailed high social integration, whereas the very transition (conversion) into a marginal religious movement must have involved a degree of status inconsistency or status dissonance. As we shall see, it is ambiguity of social status which is more a factor in several of the social tensions reflected in 1 Corinthians - including the ambiguity of social relationship between an influential figure converted under the preaching of Paul and a Paul conscious of his financial dependency on the well-to-do for hospitality.

This chapter, therefore, will concentrate on the fresh light which has been shed on 1 Corinthians from a sociological perspective. Not surprisingly its scope largely coincides with the next six chapters of the letter, since they are the ones devoted to the tensions arising from the interaction between the newly formed Christian congregation(s) and the wider community, between the Christians with their new relationships among themselves and their continuing business and social involvement in Corinthian society.

The Power of Patronage

Chapters 5–6 have always been a problem for any theory which attempts an overarching reconstruction of the situation confronting Paul in Corinth. They deal with two problems—sexual immorality within the church and Christians taking each other to court. But why do they come at this point in the sequence of the letter, between the issues raised by Chloe's people and those posed in the Corinthian letter? How are they to be explained in terms of Corinthian parties or factions, beyond indicating that the litigiousness of certain Corinthian Christians was a factor in Corinthian factionalism? Where do they fit into a background of Gnosticism or Hellenistic Judaism or pneumatic enthusiasm or power politics? Theissen (p. 97) was unable to make much fresh contribution beyond the important observation that going to law was a prerogative of the rich, since only they had the wealth or property which would be the normal subject of a lawsuit and only they had the resources to meet the expense of a lawsuit. Meeks (p. 66) qualifies the point by noting that some financial or commercial transactions would probably be involved, but that even small traders or farmers took their neighbours to court. Beyond that, however, the situation envisaged in 1 Corinthians 5–6 has remained tantalizingly obscure.

The most promising and intriguing hypothesis has recently been suggested independently, as sometimes happens, by John Chow and Andrew Clarke. Both, but Chow in particular, have drawn attention to the social importance of the power of patronage. Roman society, and we must bear in mind that Corinth was a Roman (re)foundation, was largely built round a patron–client structure. In this relationship patron and client obligated themselves to each other, the patron providing financial resources, employment, protection, influence and so on, the client giving the patron his support, providing information and service and acting on the patron's behalf. The relationship was hierarchical, the patron providing access to resources (including power and influence) which otherwise would be unavailable to the client. Society was thus structured round a graduated hierarchy of patron–client ties. At the head was the emperor, patron in effect of the whole Empire, client of no man. The senior figures in the imperial administration were the emperor's clients, but in turn wielded huge patronal power within their spheres of responsibility. Their clients in turn would act as patrons to clients lower in the social order. And so on. It may be added that at the bottom of the patronage chain would come the freedman, typically the client of his former master.

So far as the study of 1 Corinthians is concerned, since patronage was endemic to the social order within which the church had to operate in Corinth, we can take it for granted that the members of the Corinthian church would function within such patronal relationships. This would affect the situation confronting Paul in two ways. One is that some of the relationships between members of the church would be those of patron and client. For example, 'Chloe's people' (1.11) may be better understood as clients to Chloe as patron, rather than as members of Chloe's household, and Fortunatus and Achaicus (16.17) could be Stephanas's two chief clients who travelled with him in that capacity. That is, in addition to tensions between those of different social order, wealth and property, there would be patron–client obligations between members which in some cases might be at odds with those between Christian brothers. In addition, members of the church would also be in patron–client relationships with individuals who were not members of the church and thus be caught in obligations which ran counter to their Christian commitment.

This brings us to Chow's second contribution. For he notes that what was in effect the social model of parties and groups as a means of analysing Corinthian factionalism is too static and fixed. The better and more flexible model is that of 'networks' which allows for individuals' involvement in more than one relationship or belonging to overlapping groups.

Thus to recognize the patronal character of Corinthian society is to recognize also that an individual would likely be involved in a number of different relationships, or a 'network' of relationships—in particular at one and the same time the same person a patron to one and a client to another. When we add that conversion to Christianity, involving as it did a social transition, could also be understood as the convert becoming client to a new patron, we can see at once a further dimension to the slogans on 1.12. And Paul's counsel to the Corinthians to subject themselves to such as Stephanas (16.16) can be seen as an attempt to marshall the Corinthians into a patronal relationship more amenable to Paul's own concept of discipleship and church. The network model also gives another slant to Meeks's idea of status inconsistency, since Paul's role as church founder meant a reversal of roles, for example, in effect both patron and client to Gaius at one and the same time (1.14; Rom. 16.23).

We must return to some of these matters later. For the moment it is the possibilities which the patronal thesis of Chow and Clarke opens up for our understanding of 1 Corinthians 5–6 which demand attention.

The problem confronted in 1 Corinthians 5 has always been something of a puzzle. It is not simply the character of the behaviour condemned—a member of the church living with his father's wife (5.1). It is rather that the conduct seems to have gone without comment within the Corinthian congregation itself. The most popular solution to date had been that this was seen by other Corinthians as an example of their spiritual liberty, and therefore not to be condemned. And such a solution works quite well alongside the further example of immorality (consorting with prostitutes) denounced in 6.9-20, since it was apparently justified with the slogan, 'All things are lawful for me' (6.12). Yet the immorality condemned in 5.1-5 was of a kind 'not found even among the Gentiles' (5.1), so that it remains a surprise that no voice of protest had been raised by the other Corinthian Christians, not even, it would seem, by those who would normally have taken Paul's line.

The solution of Chow and of Clarke is attractively simple. They suggest that the reason for the silence of the Christian community on such outrageous behaviour is that the man involved was a rich patron (Chow, pp. 139-40; Clarke, ch. 7). It was his social prestige and power which kept the members of the Corinthian church silent. Some of them may have been bound to him as his clients. To offend such a one could have entailed serious social consequences. Moreover a new movement whose legal status was still unclear (did the church have legal status as a synagogue or club—*collegium*?) would be particularly vulnerable if it depended for its very existence on the protection and benefaction of a patron whose word carried great power in the legal or social establishment of Corinth. Certainly when Paul talks of arrogance in 5.2 we may well envisage a congregation whose quiet acquiescence to such behaviour Paul sees as reflecting the arrogance of a powerful figure able to act in such disregard for established morality. Paul's response (expel him!) shows that he was not going to allow the privilege and even the power of status to disregard or ride roughshod over fundamental principles of ethical conduct.

Equally speculative but equally informative is the patronal hypothesis in regard to the second issue addressed in 1 Corinthians 5–6—that of litigation between members of the Corinthian church (Chow, pp. 123-30; Clarke, ch. 5). Some have suggested that the legal dispute concerned the offence of incest in 1 Corinthians 5. But Clarke notes that the description in 6.2 of 'a trivial case' indicates a civil rather than a criminal case (referring particularly to Winter, '1 Cor. 6.1-8'). And Chow notes that the term used in 6.4 (*biōtika*, 'everyday matters') covers a range of subjects including material possessions or property. Moreover the fact that Paul immediately goes on to set (such) wrongdoing in antithesis to inheriting the kingdom of God (6.9) suggests that the particular case in mind was a dispute over inheritance (a prominent subject of litigation under Roman law), the plaintiff claiming to have been defrauded of his rights (of property or inheritance) (6.7-8). Likewise the ironic plea for a wise man to decide the matter within the congregation (6.5) suggests that the plaintiff numbered himself among the minority wise (1.26), which, as we have already seen from 1.26-29, means also those of high social status. Since the legal system of the

time markedly favoured those of higher status against those
of lower rank (see Clarke, pp. 62-68), all the circumstances
of the case in Corinth would be satisfied if we envisage a
wealthy patron taking a fellow believer (one of the foolish,
weak or socially despised of 1.27-28) to court over some
disputed inheritance. Paul's response is again strong: either
6.4 is a question (the usual view), in which case 'those least
esteemed by the church' (the magistrates) indicates a defiant
reversal of values; or 6.4 is an exhortation to 'appoint
as judges even those of low esteem in the church' (Clarke,
p. 70), an equally defiant reversal of the social values of the
wider society.

Whatever the precise facts of the case there can be no
question but that a serious rupture within the congregation
was involved, and it is hard to doubt that social wealth and
power were important factors both fuelling the hostility and
enabling the one who thought he had been wronged to take
the matter to court. As in 2.6-16, where Paul posed the alternative of pneumatic wisdom against the wisdom of word and
of the world, so here he encourages the congregation to
expect one of its members to be granted the wisdom (6.5)
necessary to resolve the dispute without recourse to outside
authorities.

Household Affairs

1 Corinthians 7 is something of an exception in recent scholarship on 1 Corinthians, for the questions regarding it
remain more or less as they always were and little new light
has been shed on them by new approaches. For example, the
recognition that 7.1b is probably a quotation from the
Corinthians' letter ('It is well for a man not to touch a
woman') is old and well established; but the meaning of
'virgin' in 7.25-38 (unmarried daughter, spiritual partner,
engaged woman) remains a matter of dispute.

One possible ray of light, however, may come from the fact
that the passage is the closest parallel we have in the undis-
puted Pauline letters to the *Haustafeln* (household rules) of
Col. 3.18–4.1 and Eph. 5.22–6.9. As David Balch in particular has made clear, these household codes reflect a familiar

pattern in Greco-Roman writing on household management, where the concerns are very much the same, on how the relations between husbands and wives, fathers and children, masters and slaves should be ordered as the basis of an orderly society. It is noticeable in 1 Corinthians 7 that the same sequence of relationships appear—husbands and wives (7.1-16), children (7.14) and slaves (7.21-24); and that the moderating ideals are those cherished more widely for their social value—self-control (7.5, 9) and good order (7.35). There are obvious differences, but the circle of concern remains the same (see also Balch, '1 Cor. 7.32-35').

The parallel is instructive not so much for the similarities as for the differences. For the later *Haustafeln* have in view established households, and the concern is much the same as in wider society: to sustain these households in orderly fashion. So much so that the language is conventional—wives to be subject to husbands, children to obey parents, slaves to obey masters—even if the motivation is distinctively Christian ('in the Lord'). They can properly be classified as society-conforming.

In 1 Corinthians 7, however, we are confronted at every turn with relationships in transition, as the new loyalty (to Christ) of one or both of the marriage (or would-be marriage) partners causes them to contemplate the implications of that new loyalty for these relationships and for their children, and the slaves contemplate its implications for their status. If married, should their sexual responsibilities to each other change? If unmarried, should they be married? If married to an unbeliever, should they separate? Should slaves remain slaves or grasp at the chance of freedom? In other words, where the later *Haustafeln* deal primarily with households conceived as within the new society of the church, and can therefore present them as such as contributing to a stable wider society, 1 Corinthians 7 deals with a situation where the new relationships of church were cutting across the more established relationships of the wider society (in a way analogous to 6.1-8) and causing friction and uncertainty as to role and responsibility for which conventional counsel was inadequate.

In this way we can set the issues discussed in 1 Corinthians 7 within a wider social framework (the role of the household within society) and refuse to reduce them to a sequence of problems of personal morality for different individuals. The advantage of so doing is that we can understand better why it is that Paul, normally so sure-footed on questions of moral behaviour (cf. 1 Cor. 5–6!), appears in 1 Corinthians 7 as much less confident and as issuing essentially *ad hoc* advice. It is not simply that he thought the time short or the priorities of mission compelling—though both of these are undoubtedly factors (7.29-35). It is also that the emergence of a new social grouping (the church) was cutting across and grating against older social groupings (the household) and thus posing problems which the Corinthian Christians apparently put at the head of their worry list and which Paul could only deal with in an *ad hoc* manner. The point may be characterized by noting that the same word is used in 7.34 as in 1.13 in countering the factionalism of the Corinthians: 'Is Christ divided?' (1.13); 'the married man is concerned with the things of the world (could we say, 'the affairs of the wider society'?) and is divided' (7.33-34). It is the dividedness between belonging to the church and belonging to the world which Paul found more difficult to give a clear answer to than the dividedness of Corinthian factionalism (see also MacDonald).

This larger social context may be a clue to understanding one much controverted passage—the advice Paul gives to slaves (7.21-24; Bartchy, pp. 6-7 contains an impressive list of those holding to the alternative views). The passage is a sensitive one since it has provided the basis for a Christian doctrine of a social position as a 'calling' (7.20). The problem is the ambiguity of the word 'calling' (as in 1.26). Did Paul encourage his Corinthian converts to see their position in society as a calling to which (and in which) they should remain faithful (so e.g. NRSV on 7.20-21, 24)? Or did he restrict the concept of calling to Christian conversion, to the new status and role which conversion opened up to slave and free alike? Scott Bartchy has argued strongly in favour of the latter. And in the context as illumined above, where the thought is not of conformity to current social mores (as in the later *Haustafeln*) but of the modifications on these mores which transition into the new social grouping (the church) may entail, the weight of probability falls on the second alternative: 'If you can gain your freedom, avail yourself of the opportunity' (NRSV margin).

For many the thrust of Paul's teaching in ch. 7 is summed up in the *hōs mē* ('as though not') of 7.29-31, a *locus classicus* in patristic and reformation exegesis in expounding the appropriate mode of Christian existence in the world (repeatedly cited by Rudolf Bultmann in particular). The consensus view is that Paul was directly influenced by an eschatological consciousness of the shortness and so urgency of the time (7.29; cf. particularly *6 Ezra* = 2 Esdras 16.40-44). Vincent Wimbush, however, argues that there is a shift in thought in 7.31b ('the present form of this world is passing away') to the *transience* of the world and its distracting power. Just as earlier the call to 'remain' (7.20, 24) was intended not to support the *status quo* but to *relativize* the importance of all worldly conditions and relationships, so the *hōs mē* calls for an inner detachment from the world, a spiritual though not physical distancing from the world. In Paul's perspective this would most likely involve a degree of asceticism for those whose goal is to please the Lord. The shift in nuance is importance, since it means that the ethical principle emerging from these verses is not dependent solely on Paul's sense of the imminence of the end. The primacy of the affairs of the Lord, rather than the imminence of his coming, is what relativizes (not abolishes or devalues) all other concerns.

The Strong and the Weak

The social dimensions of the chief problem tackled in 1 Corinthians 8–10 are obvious. It is the problem caused by members of the new Christian community who ate food which had been offered to an idol (those whose conscience is strong). By so doing they encouraged other believers who thought that food sacrificed to idols was contaminated (those whose conscience is weak) to act against their conscience (by eating such food themselves), that is, to act in a self-destructive way (8.11)—whether by denying their (albeit weak) faith, or by putting themselves back into partnership with or under control by demons (10.20-21).

As in other issues tackled in 1 Corinthians, the social dimensions of 1 Corinthians 8–10 were largely lost to sight for much of the century, partly because the passage was so important in clarifying the other questions which dominated the then debates among commentators. Do the tensions between chs. 8 and 10 and the somewhat awkward insertion of ch. 9 between them indicate that different letters have been amalgamated? Was the problem of idol food primarily a Jew/Gentile issue, with the Cephas party prominent among the 'weak'? Should we classify the 'strong' as Gnostics since 'knowledge' was their watchword (8.1, 7, 10, 11)? Certainly on the second question it is hard to avoid the conclusion that the motivations of the 'weak' were primarily Jewish in character. In the ancient world the abhorrence of idolatry was quintessentially and distinctively Jewish, and it is that abhorrence which dominates the discussion, both the fear of the 'weak' (8.1, 4, 7, 10) and also Paul's response (10.7, 14, 19-22); hence also the concluding concern in 10.32. That, however, does not imply that all the weak were Jewish Christians or that all the strong were Gentiles (Paul numbered himself among the strong, 8.8; 10.25-26), so that the focus on the Jewish/Gentile question and on particular parties is less valuable. Similarly with the Gnostic hypothesis, since again Paul agrees with the central claim of the *gnosis* (8.1, 4).

In this case too it was Theissen who brought to renewed attention the social dimensions of the issue. He argues that the weak would probably belong among the lower strata of society, who could not afford to include meat in their routine diet. The only times they could hope to eat meat were the public distributions of meat at public ceremonies. These would also be religious ceremonies, so that the meat would have been dedicated to the particular god(s) who presided over the ceremonies. This meant that the connection between meat-eating and idol-meat was unavoidable for the weak, for whom the solution would be to avoid eating meat altogether.

The other side of the problem was that Christians of high

social status would have been more integrated into the public life of their town or city and would find it difficult to avoid participating in public functions and feasts where idol meat would be served. Erastus, the 'city treasurer', might well have jeopardized his public position if he had rejected all invitations to such occasions (Theissen, p. 130). In other words, as the weak can be identified with those of lower social status, so the strong (the knowledgeable one who eats in an idol temple, 8.10) can be largely identified with those of higher social status. Their better education undergirds their liberal attitude. Theissen speaks of them as 'Gnostic Christians', but his case is independent of an identification of the strong as Gnostics.

Paul's response, Theissen notes, is addressed almost exclusively to the strong (p. 137). In it he sides with the weak to the extent of banning participation in public festivals where the poorer members of the church might see fellow Christians apparently honouring idols and associating with demons by their participation in such a public banquet (8.10; 10.14-22). But otherwise he sides with the strong in encouraging them to join in private meals (where meat served would routinely have been sacrificed in temples before being sold in the market place) without asking questions (10.23-30). Theissen classifies this as 'love-patriarchalism' which 'allows social inequalities to continue but transfuses them with a spirit of concern, of respect, and of personal solicitude' (p. 139).

Theissen's contribution has again been salutary, and though Wendell Willis, despite covering the same ground, hardly notes it and ignores the issue of rich and poor in the Corinthian situation, it is not to be doubted that social status was a major factor in the tensions within the Corinthian congregation over idol meat. To be sure, Meeks's strictures are again to the point (Meeks, p. 70). The straightforward identification of the strong as those who enjoyed high social integration has to be questioned. A knowledge which dismissed idols as 'nothing' would not necessarily foster good social relations with those who respected the gods, even if only in a formal way. And well-to-do Gentiles who had been God-fearers before they became Christians would have found themselves pulled in two directions, between the Jewish abhorrence of idolatry which had attracted them and their position in society. In other words, the tensions of social dissonance and status inconsistency should be allowed a place in the analysis also (cf. and contrast Barclay).

Moreover it is important to recognize that Paul does not tackle the problem simply as one of social dissension. As Bruce Winter ('1 Cor. 8-10') has noted, at the heart of both the self-justification of the 'knowalls' and of Paul's response lies the issue of religious pluralism and the reality therein involved (8.4-6; 10.19-21). Nor does Theissen's solution of 'love-patriarchalism' reckon sufficiently with the dynamic of the church's own community formation, where genuine love for those who had made the same commitment (brothers) and shared concern for the church's upbuilding could be appealed to with confidence (8.1, 3; 8.11-13; 8.1, 10 and 10.23). Once again it is the theological consideration, in this case of the community as Christ's body (10.17) and therefore of their responsibility for one another (cf. 12.25-26), which becomes determinative in resolving the problem of social relationships.

Paul's Liberty and Social Dependence

Between chs. 8 and 10, the subject of the preceding section, comes ch. 9, which seems at first to disrupt a unified discussion regarding idol meat. The chapters, however, are clearly linked by the overlapping themes of 'authority/right' (*exousia*, 8.9 and 9.4-6, 12, 18) and 'freedom' (*eleutheria*, 9.1, 19 and 10.29). As part of his discussion of liberty of conscience (but that sounds far too individualistic) in social behaviour Paul presents himself as an example of someone who has rights but who nevertheless foregoes them. In this way he can serve as an example to the strong.

The subject at issue in ch. 9 is the financial support which Paul, as missionary and church founder, might have claimed from the church he had founded. Why does Paul raise it at this point? Some have suggested that this was one of the questions put to Paul by the Corinthians, but there is no indication of that here. Others say that he was responding to a charge of inconsistency, but that aspect of the subject is introduced only towards the end of the discussion (9.19). If we give primary attention to what Paul actually says, the obvious conclusion to draw is that Paul chose to introduce the subject himself. Nevertheless the subject was obviously a sensitive one; the possibility of financial irregularity or scope for sharp practice when money is involved have always tended to arouse suspicions among the suspicious or disaffected.

Gerd Theissen again added a new twist to the debate. He builds out from the evidence in 2 Corinthians 10–13 that Paul was in competition with other missionaries, and that Paul was charged with refusing to accept support as did the other missionaries (2 Cor. 11.7-11). From this he deduces that what was in conflict here were two different ideals of missionary work. One was the itinerant charismatic, who depended entirely on the hospitality and provision provided for him by those to whom he ministered. This piety of poverty Jesus himself had encouraged in sending out his disciples in their mission (Mk 6.7-11). And this ideal was the one cherished by the Corinthians, where the practice of charismatic poverty was seen not simply as a privilege but as an apostolic duty. The charge against Paul, then, was that he had offended against the primitive and normative Christian ideal set by Jesus himself. The other ideal was the community organizer, as represented by Paul himself. In this case the radical theocratic element ('the kingdom of God is at hand') has disappeared. Mission takes place in the context of the Hellenistic city where churches were organized more on the pattern of households, and where charismatic begging was inappropriate. In comparison with the itinerant Cynic philosopher it is not his begging which provides the parallel but his claim to liberty and self-sufficiency.

The strains in Theissen's reconstruction in this case are plain. Above all it is a dubious procedure to run 1 Corinthians 9 and 2 Corinthians 11 together as though it was self-evident that they addressed the same situation. There is in fact nothing in 1 Corinthians 9 to indicate that Paul was responding to a complaint from the Corinthians on this point, or that they were offended at his failure to accept their financial support. On the contrary, it is Paul himself who builds up the case for such support, citing both Scripture and Jesus tradition in his support (9.1-14). Only then does he explain his own practice, that is, not to accept such support, choosing rather to forego his rights and to maintain himself (9.15-18). In this way he can both present himself as a free man (9.19-23), that is by his refusal to claim his rights, and maintain the self-discipline necessary for the Christian race (9.24-27).

Ronald Hock helpfully broadens the discussion by noting that the question of what means of support was appropriate for a philosopher had been a debate of long standing. Over the centuries four options were canvassed: charging fees, entering a household as its resident intellectual, begging and working. Of the four, philosophers usually preferred charging fees or entering a household; working was the least popular option (Hock, pp. 58-59). Of these options, Paul also seems to have depended to a considerable degree on hospitality: Judge pictures Paul as moving among the urban elite, using their houses for meetings and to make contact with other well-to-do citizens (cf. already 'Scholastic Community', p. 7). But in Corinth Paul had obviously chosen the fourth option - to support himself by the work of his own hands. He explicitly rejects the alternative of charging a fee (9.18), even though he regarded the work in none too positive light (4.11-12), and despite the criticism it provoked from the Corinthians.

But if Paul actually supported himself by his physical labour as a tent-maker, two fascinating corollaries follow, not much observed prior to Hock. One is that his trade must have occupied much of his time, most of his day in fact; otherwise it would have been hard to make ends meet. Consequently, his trade must have largely determined his daily experiences and social status.

> His life was very much that of the workshop—of artisan-friends like Aquila...of leather, knives, and awls; of wearying toil; of being bent over a workbench like a slave and of working side by side with slaves...of suffering the artisans' lack of status (Hock, p. 67).

Secondly, given that so much of Paul's time would be spent at his trade in the relative quiet of a leatherworking shop, and knowing Paul's commitment to evangelism, it is probable that he used the time also to forward his missionary work. As again Hock notes: 'It is difficult to imagine Paul *not* bringing up the subject of the gospel during discussions with fellow-workers, customers, and others who entered the shop' (Hock, p. 41; see also p. 17 above). Once again all this is speculative, but failure to ask how Paul's evangelism was related to his financial support simply promotes an unrealistic ideal of Paul as apostle.

Another major contribution in this area in recent years has been Peter Marshall's analysis of Paul's financial relationships with the Corinthians in terms of friendship. Marshall notes that although the common terms of friendship do not appear in Paul's letters, a number of the important conventions governing the conduct of friendships are present. Drawing on the findings of the anthropologist Marcel Mauss, he starts from the insight that in primitive societies 'gift exchange forms the whole basis of friendly relations'. To give, to accept, to return, these are the conditions of friendship. In contrast, and this is the key point of relevance for Marshall, whereas acceptance of gifts establishes friendship, refusal of gifts creates enmity. Having grounded Mauss's model in Greco-Roman writing on friendship Marshall applies it to 1 Corinthians 9 in particular (summarized on pp. 396-98).

In his initial relations with the well-to-do Corinthians Paul would have operated within the conventions of friendship, particularly in that he had depended on them for hospitality. But latterly he had refused their offer of aid, which would have provoked a hostile response, since it would be perceived as a rejection of friendship. When we include the factor of Corinthian factionalism we can see some of the reasons why Paul might have so acted. To have accepted support from one group (or individual) rather than others would have put him under obligation to a powerful benefactor. So, too, to have refused the gift would be seen as refusing the benefactor's friendship and dishonouring him. In this situation Paul would have found it almost impossible, given the complexities of friendship conventions and the emerging Corinthian factionalism, to have conducted himself **without** causing offence to one or other.

The chief problem with Marshall's monograph is his

attempt to use 'friendship' as the overarching motif in a
study which also analyses concepts of flattery, *hubris* and
freedom. An important issue which remains unclear is
whether the relationship between Paul and the wealthy
Corinthians was perceived as between people of mutually
respected rank, in which the offering of a gift would be an
expression of a desire for friendship, not excluding the obligations of friendship. Or whether it was perceived as between
persons of status and Paul as a social inferior, in which the
effect of accepting the gift would be to bind Paul as client to
patron. Nevertheless, Marshall has opened up another valuable perspective which sheds light on the complexities of
social relationships and the sensitivities of the well-to-do in
Corinth. Moreover Paul's awareness of such conventions and
occasional allusions to them helps explain why Paul responds
as he does. For in effect, he attempts to shift the sensitive
issue of financial support away from such conventions and to
resolve them in his own, Christian terms. First by setting out
his rights as an apostle (not as friend or client), and then by
justifying his refusal of these rights in terms of gospel liberty
and self-discipline.

Finally, in regard to a passage which has attracted a
surprising amount of attention in recent years, we should
mention the study of Dale Martin. He focuses on Paul's use
of slave language in 7.22 and 9.19. His principal observation
is that the metaphor of slave by no means necessarily
denoted lack of authority. Slaves could hold positions of
considerable responsibility, and a slave of an important
person in government or business could, when representing
his master, wield considerable power. Consequently within a
patronal structure, 'slave of Christ' could denote a position of
authority and power and function as a designation of leadership. And though manual labour was generally regarded as
demeaning for the educated, such self-lowering was a not
uncommon part of a populist leader's appeal, as against the
benevolent patriarchal model of leadership. So Paul's self-
enslavement in 9.19 is an attempt to establish a model of
leadership, though its tactic of self-abasement stands in
contrast to Theissen's 'love-patriarchalism', and its motivation is again more theological (Christ–wisdom–crucified 'for

you') than merely tactical. But the effect, and indeed ultimate goal of Paul's rhetoric, is to challenge the alternative link between high-status and leadership within the church assumed by those who disapproved of Paul working to support himself.

Once again, whether all these observations are wholly to the point and reflect conscious or unconscious motivation on the part of Paul and the well-to-do Corinthians in particular is not the sole criterion of their value. Their value is rather in making modern exegetes and interpreters aware that there would have been dimensions like these within the social, cultural and personal constraints which shaped Paul's language and the way it would have been perceived. They also remind us that Paul's theology was rooted within living historical contexts and in constant play with social tradition and convention.

The Body and Purity

Before leaving this section of the letter we should note one other attempt to shed light on these chapters (5–10) from a social science perspective. In this case, social anthropology, and here the work of Jerome Neyrey, drawing on the seminal studies of Mary Douglas. Douglas's basic insight is the correlation between the social body (culture, system) and the physical body (so also in Meeks, pp. 97-98). As the body is a bounded system, so society is defined as a body by its boundaries. More to the point, the social body has found it necessary to control its own boundaries by controlling the physical body's boundary, that is in particular, its orifices. Hence the importance in ancient societies, not least Israel, of strict rules of ritual purity regulating food, sexual activity and emissions and bodily waste. Abuse of such rules is perceived in such communities as threatening not simply the individual but society itself.

This has bearing on 1 Corinthians particularly in the extent to which the chapters following the lengthy first topic (1–4) are dominated by questions of sexual relations (5–7) and food consumption (8–10). Thus Paul's horror at the illicit sexual union (5.1) is not that simply of personal distaste for immorality as for behaviour which is socially destructive. It is a leaven which renders the rest of the community impure (5.6-8); like a bodily impurity, the sexually immoral person has to be expelled from the system otherwise his behaviour will corrupt the whole (5.9-13). In 6.12-20 Paul sees the parallel between food and sex, both bodily functions, and both capable of destroying membership of Christ and of rendering impure the body itself as temple of the Holy Spirit. In 7.1-9, 25-40 the ideal which Paul himself favours is celibacy: retaining the sexual orifices intact means undivided attention to the affairs of the Lord. And in 7.10-16 a primary concern encouraging the believer to remain married to the unbelieving spouse is that the children of the union are still holy; the unbelieving partner does not render them unclean (7.14). It is important, however, to qualify what might otherwise appear to be a rigid application of purity concerns. For in each case Paul falls over himself to avoid pressurising the Corinthians with his own personal preferences and to allow, even encourage a greater diversity of practice, in accordance with individual circumstances and cases.

With the issue of food sacrificed to idols the tie-in between purity concerns and the body is again clear. For the fear of idolatry as a Jewish concern was primarily the fear of contamination, and eating was strictly governed by taboos against unclean food; idol meat entering the body through the mouth could render spiritually unclean. Hence in 8.7 the fear of defilement, in 10.6-8 the association between idolatry, eating and drinking, and sexual immorality, and in 10.14-22 the abhorrence of any thought of partnership with idols and demons through eating and drinking. Here again the coherence and sanctified character of the social body (the church) are being safeguarded by rules restricting what may pass through the oral orifice of the physical body.

The point made by Neyrey again has validity. Not that such logic and concerns would be present to the mind of Paul or the Corinthians. It is rather that Douglas's physical body/social body correlation highlights a subconscious motivation which has exercised considerable power in religious practice. So once again the value of the exercise is not in enabling a better exegesis of Paul's conscious intention in confronting the issue as he did. It is rather that, like the other applications of social-scientific insight to the letter, the bringing of a social anthropological perspective to bear on the issues in 1 Corinthians makes us aware of how much the context of thought and behaviour was socially conditioned, and how, in particular, present as well as past religious language and ritual may be governed by unconscious taboos. The value, at the very least, is that such a heightening of awareness can enable a better informed evaluation of their continuing relevance and point.

For Further Reading

D. Balch, 'Household Codes', in *Anchor Bible Dictionary*, III, pp. 318-20 (with fuller bibliography).

—'1 Cor. 7.32-35 and Stoic Debates about Marriage, Anxiety and Distraction', *JBL* 102 (1983), pp. 429-39.

J.M.G. Barclay, 'Thessalonica and Corinth: Social Contrasts in Pauline Christianity', *JSNT* 47 (1992), pp. 48-74.

S.S. Bartchy, *First-Century Slavery and 1 Corinthians 7.21* (SBLDS, 11; Missoula, MT: Scholars Press, 1973).

J.K. Chow, *Patronage and Power: A Study of Social Networks in Corinth* (JSNTSup, 75; Sheffield: JSOT Press, 1992).

A.D. Clarke, *Secular and Christian Leadership in Corinth: A Socio-Historical and Exegetical Study of 1 Corinthians 1–6* (Leiden: Brill, 1993).

M. Douglas, *Natural Symbols: Explorations in Cosmology* (London: Barrie & Jenkins, 1973).

R.F. Hock, *The Social Context of Paul's Ministry: Tentmaking and Apostleship* (Philadelphia: Fortress Press, 1980).

E.A. Judge, *The Social Pattern of Christian Groups in the First Century* (London: Tyndale Press, 1960).

—'The Early Christians as a Scholastic Community', *JRH* 1 (1960–61), pp. 4-15, 125-37.

M.Y. MacDonald, 'Women Holy in Body and Spirit: The Social Setting of 1 Corinthians 7', *NTS* 36 (1990), pp. 161-81.

A.J. Malherbe, *Social Aspects of Early Christianity* (Baton Rouge: Louisiana State University Press, 1977).

P. Marshall, *Enmity in Corinth: Social Conventions in Paul's Relations with the Corinthians* (WUNT, 2.23; Tübingen: Mohr, 1987).

D.B. Martin, *Slavery as Salvation: The Metaphor of Slavery in Pauline Christianity* (New Haven, CT: Yale University Press, 1990).

W.A. Meeks, *The First Urban Christians: The Social World of the Apostle Paul* (New Haven, CT: Yale University Press, 1983).

J.H. Neyrey, 'Perceiving the Human Body: Body Language in 1 Corinthians', in his *Paul in Other Words: A Cultural Reading of his Letters* (Louisville: Westminster Press, 1990), pp. 102-46.

G. Theissen, 'Legitimation and Subsistence: An Essay on the Sociology of Early Christian Missionaries'; 'Social Stratification in the Corinthian Community: A Contribution to the Sociology of Early Hellenistic Christianity'; 'The Strong and the Weak in Corinth: A Sociological Analysis of a Theological Quarrel', in Theissen, *The Social Setting of Pauline Christianity* (Philadelphia: Fortress Press/Edinburgh: T. & T. Clark, 1982), chs. 1–3.

W.L. Willis, *Idol Meat in Corinth: The Pauline Argument in 1 Corinthians 8 and 10* (SBLDS, 68; Chico, CA: Scholars Press, 1985).

V.L. Wimbush, *Paul the Worldly Ascetic: Response to the World and Self-Understanding according to 1 Corinthians 7* (Macon GA: Mercer University Press, 1987).

B.W. Winter, 'Theological and Ethical Responses to Religious Pluralism— 1 Corinthians 8-10', *TynBul* 41.2 (1990), pp. 209-26.

—'Civil Litigation in Secular Corinth and the Church: The Forensic Background to 1 Corinthians 6.1-8', *NTS* 37 (1991), pp. 559-72.

5

BETWEEN CHURCH AND GOD:
PROBLEMS OF WORSHIP AND BELIEF:
1 CORINTHIANS 11–16

AT 11.2 PAUL SHIFTS his focus from external to internal relations. It would be incorrect to say that at this point he turned away from the problems of the church's interaction with the wider world and to its internal problems. For the problems confronted in chs. 5–10 were as much to do with internal disagreements as with what conduct and relationships in the wider community were appropriate for believers. And in chs. 11–15 a central consideration throughout is the impression made on their neighbours by the believers' behaviour when they came together as church and the consequences for their evangelistic witness to their neighbours. And questions of social status remain important in this section. Nevertheless, Paul's concern in chs. 11–15 is taken up not so much with the shifting boundaries between church and world, as in chs. 5–10, as with the shifting relationships within the Corinthian church as exposed particularly by their worship.

He deals first with the conduct of women prophets (11.2-16), and then with the very unsatisfactory conduct of the common meal and the Lords' Supper (11.17-34). A lengthy discussion of spiritual gifts and the exercise of prophecy and speaking in tongues in church indicates this was one of the major concerns of the Corinthians who brought up the issue in their letter to Paul (chs. 12–14). The final subject, presumably reported to Paul by the Stephanas group, is the one matter of belief which seems to have caused some confusion and argument among the Corinthians ('some of you', 15.12), namely the question of the resurrection of the dead (ch. 15). Since it is also a concern Paul shares with the Corinthians we include his instructions regarding the collection (16.1-4).

The Role of Women in Worship

1 Cor. 11.2-16 has been understood for most of Christianity's history as reinforcing the traditional status of women. To be sure, Paul envisages (some of) the Corinthian women praying and prophesying, but the concern of the passage seems primarily to hedge round this function with qualifications and restrictions. And it is the restrictions, rather than the fact of them prophesying, which seem to have made the more abiding impression. The passage begins abruptly with the first qualification, with what appears to be an unbending statement of male hierarchy—God is the head of Christ, Christ the head of man, man the head of woman. This is based on the creation account in Genesis 2 which is run together with the first creation account (Gen. 1), so that only man reflects the glory of God directly, whereas woman reflects the glory of man (11.7-9). And though the hierarchical relation is qualified by recognition that woman gives birth to man (11.12), the impression that Paul basically reaffirmed female subordination to male is hard to avoid. The second restriction is that woman should pray and prophesy only with her head covered, though the final consideration (11.14-15) left some uncertainty as to whether Paul thought long hair was a sufficient head covering in itself.

A particular problem comes with the correlation of 11.2-16 (women praying and prophesying) and 14.34-36 ('women should be silent in the churches'). It was reinforced by 1 Tim. 2.12-14, where a similar argument ('Adam was formed first, then Eve') is applied even more strongly: 'I permit no woman to teach or to have authority over a man'. But the contrast within 1 Corinthians itself was glaring enough. The natural solution to such hermeneutical difficulties in an age when scriptural authority was largely unquestioned, was to read the relatively unclear text (11.2-16) in the light of the more clear (14.34-36; 1 Tim. 2.12-14). Thus the potential of 11.2-16 for a more radical assertion of women's roles within the church was largely lost to sight, with only the uneasy compromise left that Paul must have had private and not public worship in mind in 11.2-16.

In the middle decades of the century two studies went some way to indicate that Paul's attitude may have been softer than the traditional interpretation allowed. S. Bedale argued that the word *kephale* should not be taken in the sense 'head', meaning ruler or chief person in a community, but 'head' meaning 'source' (like head of a river). 11.3 could then be taken less as an affirmation of hierarchy, though the end result might not be very different; but the debate rumbles on (see e.g. Fitzmyer, and Fee, p. 502 n. 42). Ten years later Morna Hooker provided the best answer to the puzzle of why Paul says in 11.10, 'Therefore the woman ought to have authority on her head on account of the angels'. The answer is surprisingly straightforward: if woman is the glory of man (11.7), then her head covering is to hide *man's* glory in the presence of God and his angels. 'Far from being a symbol of the woman's subjection to man, therefore, her head-covering is what Paul calls it—authority', for it thus functions as her authority to pray and prophesy before God.

More recently a different slant to the passage has been given by focusing more on 11.4 and 7. Jerome Murphy-O'Connor suggests that the problem in Corinth involved both men and women, men in that they wore their hair long, a characteristic of homosexuals, whereas women were neglecting their hair in an unfeminine way. David Gill has deduced from Roman portraiture that in Roman worship the social elite normally covered their heads. The problem would then be that the social elite within the Corinthian church were adopting pagan forms of worship. In neither case, however, does the suggestion explain the thrust of the passage and its failure to deal more specifically with the putative problem. In contrast, the concern in the passage seems to focus on the potential offence caused by women prophesying with their heads uncovered, with the references to men as a means of balancing but also of strengthening the primary argument.

However, the rising tide of feminism through the latter
half of the century has increasingly called in question the
force of Paul's argument and instruction in 11.2-16 and has
increasingly drawn attention to an unconscious patriarchalism which has shaped perception of early Christian
texts. Already this century at popular level the widescale
abandonment of head covering (hats) as a prerequisite for
women in attending public worship had attested the force of
social convention in such ecclesiastical regulations. But in
the last two or three decades scholarship has made us more
and more aware that women were not so completely subordinate in the world of the Pauline churches as had previously
been assumed. Women in fact often fulfilled important public
positions and roles as benefactors and patrons (see e.g.
Trebilco, ch. 5). Phoebe in Rom. 16.1-2 is a case in point, a
patron of the church in the Corinthian port of Cenchreae.
The persistence of translations up until recently in trans-
lating *prostatis* in Rom. 16.2 by something like 'helper' (RSV)
rather than 'patron or benefactor' equally illustrates the
unconscious patriarchalism against which feminist
hermeneutics have justifiably reacted.

The most influential contribution on this whole theme has
been that of Elisabeth Schüssler Fiorenza. In this case she
argues that Paul's wisdom christology (1.24, 30) was probably attractive to women, since divine Wisdom is a female
figure (sophia); it would certainly be consistent with the
prominence of women as prophets in Corinth, since Paul
links wisdom and pneumatic speech so closely in ch. 2. More
to the immediate point, she argues that Paul here is not
reacting to any particular abuse (as in chs. 12–14), but is
simply concerned to introduce regulations and customs
which were already being observed in other churches (11.16;
14.33). The concern focuses on the practice of (some of) the
Corinthian women prophets in leaving their hair unbound
while prophesying. Since dishevelled hair could evoke the
picture of ritual ecstasy familiar to several Greek cults, and
unbound hair was also found in the Isis cult, which had a
major centre in Corinth, the fear would be that outsiders
would think the new Christian church was simply another
ecstatic cult.

Paul's argument in 11.2-16, then, according to Fiorenza, is not for the maintenance of a 'creational' or 'symbolic' *difference* between men and women, but in favour of the custom of bound-up hair. And this not in order to restrict women prophesying, but in order that their prophesying with a 'proper' hairstyle should not be distracting. 'The goal of his argument...is not the reinforcement of gender differences but the order and missionary character of the worship community' (Fiorenza, p. 230). Even so, she puts Paul's treatment under the head of 'Pauline modifications of Galatians 3.28', the latter being, as it were, the primal vision of a church which in baptism had rendered insignificant distinctions of race, class and gender and abolished domination based on sexual divisions. There is a high degree of special pleading here, though no more than the special pleading of the older patriarchalist interpretations, but the force of her argument in regard to 11.2-16 is not dependent on the larger thesis.

The most thoroughgoing feminist reading of 1 Corinthians has been that of Antoinette Wire. She in effect takes 11.2-16 as her starting point. The passage attests to the significant presence of women prophets in the Corinthian assembly. From this she deduces that they would be involved also in the other problems and controversies Paul addresses in the letter. Therefore we should ask what would Paul be saying in each case to the women prophets. And since Paul so regularly addresses his teaching and counsel to the whole church, that must include the women prophets attested in 11.2-16. So the hypothesis is a fair one and the exercise valid, no less valid we may say than the attempt to ask how Paul would have been heard by Gnostics or by pneumatic enthusiasts or by those of high social status or by patrons, even if overstated.

With regard to 11.2-16 itself, Wire develops Fiorenza's thesis regarding Gal. 3.28. The women prophets appealed to this tradition in claiming that believers already embodied God's image in Christ. 'Not male and female' (Gal. 3.28) meant that believers have taken on a single common identity in Christ and can therefore pray and prophesy without regard to gender (Wire, p. 126). This she deduces from the unusual formulation of 11.7, that man is the image of God,

whereas usually Paul understands Christ as the image of
God and believers as reflecting or being transformed into
that image. Hence Paul's argument at this point is probably
an attempt to reaffirm a more traditional subordination of
women to men within traditional structures of marriage and
family, in reaction to the degree of independence the women
prophets were claiming.

The other feature Wire draws particular attention to is the
appeal to considerations of honour and shame (11.5-6), an
important motivation in the ancient world (Malina, ch. 2). It
is noticeable that the only other passage where Paul talks of
'shame' is 14.35. That the appeal could be made in these
terms indicates that the women were not of low social status
but would recognize and respond to such considerations.
Presumably they had thus far understood their honour in
terms of their new baptismal status in sharing Christ's
image. At the same time she notes how careful Paul is to
mark out an equivalence of responsibilities between men and
women (11.3-5, 7, 14-15), and that he refrains from the
stronger argument from shame—Eve's responsibility for the
fall (cf. 2 Cor. 11.3; 1 Tim. 2.14).

All this underlines how difficult it is to weight Paul's arguments here when the actual circumstances addressed and
the degree to which Paul's arguments are actually counter-
arguments are so indeterminate. Exegetes need to reflect
upon their own honour–shame culture with a proper leaven-
ing of humility in their findings and tentativeness in the
strictures they bring against Paul.

The particular problem of correlating 11.2-16 with 14.34-
36 has often proved too difficult for commentators, encouraging them to postulate that 14.34-35 (or 36) is an
interpolation (e.g. Conzelmann, p. 246; Fee, pp. 699-705).
However, with the text-critical case so strongly in favour of
its authenticity, it is better to take the text as it stands and
see what sense it makes. Here, as Fiorenza (pp. 230-33)
among others has pointed out, the solution probably lies in
the recognition that the instruction is directed not to all
women but to wives. The clue is given by Paul's talk of their
'being subject' and 'at home'. For on the one hand, subjection
of wife to husband is a typical feature of the later household

rules (Col. 3.18; Eph. 5.22; 1 Pet. 3.1), though here we may
also note that the context makes it parallel to the subjection
of the spirits of the prophets to the prophets (14.32). And on
the other, it is already implicit in ch. 7 that there were
unmarried women, some at least of whom would have maintained their own home (even if under the legal responsibility
of their senior male relative). Paul's concern, therefore, is
more for the good order of the household (wives seeming to
usurp the authority of their husbands by their questioning,
or so it would appear), and so also of the assembly (14.40),
than to promote a theology of women's subordination to men.

An important factor in the tensions at this point would
again be the ambiguity or dissonance of status, not least
because the church met typically in the private home. The
tensions likely to be caused by *public* gatherings in *private*
space are pointed up by Stephen Barton. Was the senior
male of the household there as *pater familias*, head of the
family? Was the woman of the household there as wife?
Could she behave in church as she did at home, where she
exercised a certain amount of authority? Or alternatively,
once in church was she in a new (Christian) family structure,
where there was no longer male and female, and so free(er)
from the authority of the *pater familias*? The tensions are
twofold - for the married woman who was both prophet and
wife, and yet had to function as prophet in a space which was
both church and home. And Paul seems to be pulled both
ways. On the one hand he acknowledges women's role as
prophets—and that must be in church; where else would
prophets prophesy, and to whom else would they prophesy
than to other believers? But at the same time, as Barton
notes, Paul's counsel seems to be socially conservative in that
he expects wives still to be wives while in church, and to
continue respecting the authority of their husbands.

Perhaps the compromise Paul expected was that while
wives who were prophets could indeed prophesy in the house
church, they should not take part in the process of evaluating
each prophecy which was the primary responsibility of the
other prophets (14.29).

Abuse of the Lord's Supper

One of the most serious problems in the view of Paul and his
informants (11.18), but not, it would appear, of the
Corinthians who wrote the letter to Paul, was the behaviour
of the Corinthians at the common meal. 11.18 is the only
time, apart from the thematic verse 1.10, that Paul speaks of
'schisms', and in 11.19 he speaks for the only time of
'factions'. Evidently the unity of the Corinthian church was
most at risk precisely because the expression of unity and of
mutual sharing (10.16-17) had become an expression of greed
and inconsiderateness (11.21). Ironically, the focus of unity
had become the focus of division - an irony often repeated in
the history of Christianity.

Traditionally the passage has been of primary importance
as being the only Pauline description of the Lord's Supper
and as the only attestation of the institution of the Eucharist
outside the Gospels. In many ecclesiastical traditions the
passage has been of supreme importance as indicating the
sacred character of the eucharistic elements and as requiring
a careful self-scrutiny by would-be communicants. The implication that ill health or even death could be a consequence of
'unworthy' eating and drinking (11.27-30) was particularly
sobering and increased the solemnity of the sacramental
occasion. On the other hand, it has been equally argued that
the sin primarily condemned in 11.29 was failure to recognize the character not so much of the bread as the body of
Christ, as of the church as the body of Christ; proper discernment of the body in this sense is what would have prevented
people acting independently of one another and without
concern for other members of the body. The point is parallel
to the emphasis on sharing the one bread in 10.16-17 as the
action which constitutes the body as one.

Such debates on emphasis and nuance continue to tax the
scholarship and wit of commentators. But the present
century has seen fresh aspects brought to the fore. Early on,
the parallel between sacrificial meals of Israel and contemporary cults in 10.18-21 invited exploration of the idea that the
Christian sacrament had been decisively influenced by the
cult meals of the pagan mysteries; Eleusis, where the famous

mysteries were celebrated, was only fourteen miles from Corinth. However, since we know so little about the mysteries and their meals (they kept their secrets well), since eating always has been such a common focus of community, and since the rationale for the Lord's Supper seems to be quite fully enough explicated from the tradition of the Last Supper inherited by Paul in and from the earliest days of the new movement, we need hardly look further for an explanation of the practice of the Pauline churches. In a recent brief review of the issue Hans-Josef Klauck points to the various analogies which may be drawn on to illuminate the Lord's Supper in Paul, but concludes that it would be a mistake to deduce that the Lord's Supper was assembled, mosaic-like, out of such elements; 'the whole remains a creative synthesis, unique and underived' (p. 74).

More recently fresh stimulus has come from the awareness that the Lord's Supper was an adaptation of the Jewish Passover. This would mean that the blessing and breaking of bread was the typical first act of the meal as a whole, while, as is explicitly stated here, the cup came 'after supper' (11.25). In other words, the Lord's Supper was itself a meal, the bread and wine beginning and completing it (see particularly Hofius, pp. 80-96). When this observation is added to the realization that the churches met in private homes, and is further linked in to the archaeological evidence of the likely sizes of such homes, the picture which emerges of the typical shared meal and sacrament becomes strikingly everyday, part of and expressive of their common life, meaning by that the lives they actually lived in the city. Robert Banks has helpfully highlighted these and other aspects of what it meant to be part of the typical Pauline church.

Gerd Theissen again opened up a new dimension to the discussion by arguing that the problem was not so much theological as social, the problems of a socially stratified community. The conflict was basically between rich and poor Christians, between those who had enough food and those who had nothing (11.22). The rich were going ahead with their meal before the poor arrived (11.33). Presumably the common meals were hosted by wealthier Christians in their own homes. But in accordance with the practice of the time those of higher social status may well have kept the best food for their social peers and provided poorer quality food for their social inferiors and clients (a good example is given in Pliny, *Epistles* 2.6). According to Theissen, Paul's solution is again along the lines of 'love-patriarchalism', leaving the wealthier to behave according to the norms of their social class in their private gatherings, but requiring them to behave as equal members of the body of Christ at the Lord's Supper itself.

Observations of two other recent contributors already referred to in Chapter Four should also be noted. Meeks extends Theissen's analysis by drawing attention to the boundary function of the Lord's Supper (Meeks, pp. 159-60). It was the exclusivity of this central act of community (10.21) which would have marked out the distinctiveness of the Christian practice in the eyes of their neighbours. And Neyrey argues that the selfish behaviour of the Corinthian rich was polluting the Eucharist and rendering it ineffective; it lost its holiness (Neyrey, p. 124). A more appropriate comment, however, would have been that the holy, when infringed, does not become ineffective, but rather its power for wholeness becomes a power of destruction (11.30). Gill adds the note that famine may have been a factor (51 CE had been a famine year); this, of course, would have exacerbated social tensions, with the social elite more able to secure scarce provisions.

Most recently Peter Lampe has drawn attention to another feature of ancient entertaining. According to the tradition of the *eranos*, which he translates roughly as 'pot-luck dinner', either each participant brought and ate his or her own food, or all the provisions were put on a common table. The problem at Corinth would be that some came early and began eating before the others. Those arriving later would probably have had insufficient time or money to prepare enough food for themselves. Arriving late they would find that most of the more expensive and substantial food brought by the wealthier early-comers would already have been eaten. In addition, latecomers might well find there was insufficient room in the *triclinium* (dining room) and would have to sit in the atrium (see above p. 17 and Murphy-O'Connor, *Corinth*, pp. 168-69). The picture is again speculative but persuasive. It should occasion no surprise that a movement of such religious motivation operated within social conventions which were at odds with its primary inspiration without apparently being aware of the fact. The same thing has happened often enough within the history of Christianity for it to be unremarkable in this case.

Lampe also draws on the tradition of the Greco-Roman dinner party falling into two phases—a 'first table', during which several courses were served, followed by a break and afterwards a symposium (drinking party) at a 'second table', often with newly arrived guests, at which some food and desserts were served. He suggests that the problems in the Corinthian church were caused by the richer Christians maintaining the practice of a first table and regarding the eucharistic meal as the second table alone (Lampe, p. 40). This makes some sense of the evidence in 1 Corinthians, not least in explaining how the shared bread could come at the beginning of a single meal when people were arriving at different times after it had started. The flaw is that Paul speaks of only one common meal (the Lord's Supper), and the practice he rebukes is not that of a preceding shared meal but of some eating their own meal while allowing others to go hungry (11.21).

So the precise details remain obscure. Nevertheless, it can hardly be doubted that the problems in the Corinthian assembly were caused not by theological disagreement but by social status and convention running counter to the more egalitarian ethos of Pauline Christianity.

Charisma and Confusion

Although the treatment of charisms (*charismata*, spiritual gifts) in chs. 12–14 takes up more verses than any other subject in 1 Corinthians, it has excited less scholarly interest. This is partly because the situation envisaged at Corinth is much clearer and Paul's response more internally coherent than any other in the letter. And partly because for the great bulk of Christian history there has been a wide-

spread assumption that the charisms spoken of had been
given only to the apostolic age, so that Paul's treatment was
a historical curiosity more than an issue of living interest for
the church (1 Cor. 13 always excepted). Thus his practical
exposition of what it means for the church to be Christ's body
is powerful but uncontroversial (12.14-26), and his argument
for the superiority of prophecy over glossolalia (speaking in
tongues) is so thorough as to require little clarification or
elaboration (ch. 14). The only room for much disagreement in
ch. 14 was on the nature of glossolalia (see further below), on
the puzzle of how an unknown tongue can be a sign for unbelievers (14.22, probably a sign of judgment as the context
implies), and on the question of whether 14.34-35(36) is an
interpolation (referred to above, pp. 73-74).

History of religions research at the beginning of the
century made scholars more aware that charismatic
phenomena and ecstatic behaviour were common features of
many cults of the time. 12.2 almost certainly refers to such
cultic madness, such as was a feature of the Dionysiac festivals familiar throughout Greece ('carried away to dumb
idols'). It is therefore a fair inference from 12.2 that at least
some of the Corinthian believers had personally participated
in such uninhibited celebrations. Terence Paige suggests that
all that is in view in 12.2 is participation in a cultic religious
procession, but why such an allusion would be made in a
context where the talk is of spiritual gifts and experiences of
inspiration is not clear. The problem for Paul seems rather to
have been that the behaviour in the Corinthian assembly too
often gave the same impression of uninhibited behaviour
justified as experience of the Spirit: 14.12, 'zealous for spirits'
(not 'spiritual gifts', as most translations render), that is, for
experiences of possession or inspiration; 14.23, 'they will say,
"You are mad"', that is, like the Dionysiac revellers, out of
control. This confirms the conclusion from Chapter Three
that the principal influence at this point anyway was most
likely from Spirit enthusiasts rather than a group properly to
be called Gnostic.

How this last finding correlates with the repeated findings
of earlier sections, that social status and stratification were
major factors in the Corinthian divisions, is less clear. It

could be, of course, that those of higher status regarded a leading role in a Dionysiac-like festival as a matter of prestige and honour, so that manifestation of the Spirit's gifts was a much coveted experience among the well-to-do. Alternatively we may need to recall rather that the Corinthian letter does not seem to have raised some of the most sensitive social tensions (1–4; 5–6; 11.17-34). So the likelihood that the issue of charisms was raised in the letter (12.1) may indicate that it was leaders of higher social status who raised it and that they were concerned about the unfortunate impression being given by the enthusiasts. Certainly the implication of 12.2 is that experiences of unrestrained ecstasy should be regarded as belonging to the past; and for outsiders or unbelievers to say 'You are mad' would evidently not be a compliment in the eyes of Paul's correspondents either. We should probably see here, therefore, further evidence that the Corinthian factionalism was quite diverse and probably cut across social distinctions.

The main interpretative issue at the turn of the century, however, was the debate about charisma and office. Was the church initially a charismatic movement, as 1 Corinthians 12–14 implies? And did the idea of legal structure and church office only emerge in the process of institutionalization? An earlier sociological influence on New Testament study, that of Max Weber, is visible at this point (see Chapter Six below). Or does Paul's setting out a hierarchy of ministries in 12.28 ('first apostles, second prophets, third teachers') indicate a clear organizational structure from the first? Or, alternatively, were there different structures for the churches in different regions? The discussion is, of course, much broader than 1 Corinthians, but it was 1 Corinthians 12–14 which gave it its decisive impetus. A particularly influential exposition of the charismatic character of the Pauline churches from the Protestant side has been that of Eduard Schweizer, while Hans Küng well expresses the balance between the two emphases which has been so influential on Vatican II and post-Vatican Catholic ecclesiology.

The emergence and growth of the Pentecostal churches in the first half of the century and then of the charismatic movement in the second half has given a further boost to interest in these chapters of 1 Corinthians. The possibility that 12.13 had in view the spiritual experience of baptism in the Spirit rather than, or perhaps as the heart of the sacrament of baptism, was pushed with some vigour. The old view that the charisms were only for the apostolic age, or the period prior to the New Testament, could be now completely discounted, and 13.10 freed from a tendentious interpretation in favour of that view. And the value of glossolalia became as much contested as it seems to have been in Corinth, with Pentecostals emphasizing Paul's own appreciative use of the gift, presumably in private (14.18), over against his overall strictures on its use in the assembly (14.6-23). An early fruit of the charismatic renewal was the commentary on these chapters by the Lutheran charismatic, Arnold Bittlinger. And one of the recent major commentaries on the letter as a whole comes from the pen of a Pentecostal, Gordon Fee.

In sympathetic critique I have made two points worth some consideration (*Jesus and the Spirit*). One is the basic definition of charism (*charisma*) as the embodiment and manifestation of grace (*charis*). This reinforces the recognition that the list of charisms in 12.4-11 is most unlikely to be exhaustive (*the* spiritual gifts), but is simply an example of typical charisms particularly relevant to the Corinthian situation. The point is that *any* word or deed which embodies grace or makes it present to others is properly speaking a charism. The same insight also underlines the 'event' character of a charism; it is the actual word or deed itself which embodies the grace, brings the grace to manifest expression, is the charism. A charism is thus not a potential within a person (properly speaking grace is the potential), and to speak of 'having a charism' is a loose form of speech (otherwise, e.g., Carson, pp. 21-22). The point is clearest in the description of worship in 14.26-32 and in the participles of the parallel list in Rom. 12.6-8.

My other point is the importance of what might be called the checks and balances which Paul emphasizes in relation to the two most prominent gifts. Speaking in tongues must be accompanied by interpretation (14.13-15); just as prophecy be accompanied by 'discernment of spirits' (12.10; cf. 2.13-15), or evaluation of what is said (14.29; cf. 1 Thess. 5.19-22). The role of interpretation in relation to tongues has been observed within Pentecostal circles; less so the 'control' effect of 'testing' prophecy. The need for such evaluation as a hermeneutical principle, in effect the answer to the danger of false prophecy as recognized throughout the history of biblical prophecy (e.g. Deut. 13.1-3; Jer. 28; Mic. 5.4-8; 1 Jn 4.1-3), is also subverted by Wayne Grudem with his arbitrary distinction between primary (canonical) prophecy ('authority of general content') and Corinthian prophecy as a secondary type of prophecy ('authority of actual words').

Another issue was raised by the New English Bible's translation of 'tongues' (12.10; 13.8; 14.2 etc.) as 'the gift of ecstatic utterance', 'tongues of ecstasy', 'the language of ecstasy', and so on. It has to be said that as a translation it is somewhat questionable (Revised English Bible has abandoned it for the most part). The term itself simply means 'language' (we still use 'tongue' in that sense), and Paul probably thought that the gift was indeed of a language, albeit the language of heaven (14.2; cf. 13.1); the experience of a heavenly journey in which one spoke the language of angels was quite well known in some circles (e.g. *T. Job* 48–50). On the other hand, we have already noted the clear implication that ecstatic experience was known to and coveted by some at least of the Corinthians (12.2; 14.12, 23). Yet, even so, Paul assumes that tongues-speakers have a degree of control over their gift; if no interpreter/translator is present they should keep silent (14.28). Perhaps, then, we have to distinguish between 'hot' ecstasy and 'cool' ecstasy.

And if the question is open with regard to tongues, then it is even more so in the case of prophecy. It too is 'ecstatic' in a technical sense: words given from 'without' (*ekstasis*, standing outside of oneself), but the mind is still the medium and monitor (14.13-19), and Paul emphasizes that 'the spirits of prophets are subject to prophets' (14.32). A recent article by Terence Callan argues that 'prophet' covers a range of functions in Greek, and that in Paul it is not ecstatic, that is, not accompanied by a trance (unlike glossolalia).

The overall and abiding impression, however, is of the

vitality of the Corinthian worship, with 14.26 as the nearest
thing we have to a description of first generation Christian
worship. Those who wish to make 14.40 the norm for all
worship should remember what manner of church it was
addressed to.

The Resurrection of the Dead and the Destruction of Death

The only other major problem Paul seems to have been
confronted with at Corinth was uncertainty or actual dispute
as to what their common gospel actually gave and promised.
As already noted in Chapter Three, the issue was probably
about the resurrection of the dead (15.12), whether there was
still a future resurrection to be awaited by believers, and if
so, what kind of body could it possibly involve (15.35). As
with chs. 12–14, once the Gnostic hypothesis has been
discounted, it seems hard to locate this particular questioning or dispute into the factionalism previously discussed.
Whereas other strong christological sections are thoroughly
integrated into arguments over wisdom and knowledge,
clearly involving social factors and tensions (1.17–2.16; 8.1-6;
10.1–11.1), there are no hints of such dimensions here. 15.8
could allude to a jibe against Paul ('the abortion') by those
who thought more highly of Cephas; baptism for the dead
(15.29) could possibly be related to social prestige; and the
attitude of 15.32b sounds more that of the well-to-do. But
little is made of any of this in terms similar to those used
earlier, and the rhetoric for the most part seems to be less
targeted against particular individuals, the questions raised
by a few providing more an occasion for Paul to engage in
some theologizing.

This is, in fact, the most striking feature of the passage. It
is the most sustained theological section in the whole letter—
almost as though Paul had decided that before he closed the
letter he would move on from the seemingly endless practical
issues to a major theological discourse. Particularly striking
is the care Paul takes in introducing and building up to the
actual theme of the chapter, by at once, without other reference, recalling his audience to the gospel he had first

preached and its authentication. Evidently it was not a matter pressed upon him by the Corinthians themselves, but in a report brought to him verbally (15.12) he saw an opportunity to develop an important aspect of his gospel, perhaps more thoroughly than he had had occásion to do before.

The passage does, however, fit more coherently into the ongoing argument and concern of 1 Corinthians than is usually recognized. For in this final section Paul, as it were, turns away from the interface between the Corinthian church and the secular community in which it was situated, and away also from the internal factionalism of the church as such, and focuses rather on the church's interface with heaven. This dimension of the Corinthians' existence had in effect been a subplot all along: the contrast between the wisdom of the world and the wisdom of God, the wisdom of rhetoric and the persuasive power of the Spirit, the hidden mysteries decreed before the ages (chs. 1–2); the promised day of judgment, talk of life or death, things present or things to come (ch. 3); the Lord's coming in apocalyptic disclosure, and the apostles as the last act on the stage of history—a spectacle to angels (ch. 4); believers judging angels, inheriting the kingdom and their bodies promised resurrection as temples of the Holy Spirit (ch. 6); the form of the world passing away (7.31); and so on. Particularly noticeable has been the frequent allusion to hostile powers: the rulers of this age (2.8), Satan as a power to be feared (5.5; 7.5), many gods and many lords (8.5), demons (10.20-21), potentially threatening angels (11.10) and potentially deceptive spirits (12.10; 14.12).

It is this dimension to which Paul now turns, as Andrew Lincoln particularly has recognized, and for the first time gives it his undivided attention. To be sure, he had started his letter to the Corinthians with this wider dimension in view, in the opening contrasts between the different wisdoms. However, it would easily have become lost to sight in the finer detail of particular crises and practical guidelines for their behaviour on the interface with the world and when they came together as church. But now as the climax to the whole he brings this subplot to the fore and indicates what the final solution is to the hostile powers which still influence their present conduct. The issue focuses in the chiefest of these, death.

It is important, then, to realize that the question dealt with in 1 Corinthians 15 is not the resurrection, far less the resurrection of Jesus. Rather, as Martinus de Boer has clearly seen, 'the fundamental issue is...death itself' (p. 105). To be more precise, the theme is the resurrection *of the dead* (the phrase is repeated 13 times); and the point to which the chapter drives is not the resurrection of the body as such, but the conquest of death, the last enemy (15.26, 54-56). In their too casual contact with the world and their spiritual enthusiasm, or enthusiasm for spirits, the Corinthians were in effect assuming that there were no powers, no realities other than the risen Christ, which could undermine their present status (cf. 4.8). That was why resurrection of the dead, as a process of salvation still to be completed (cf. 15.1-2), was so meaningless to some of them (15.12); the issue of what body the resurrected dead would have (15.35) was not at the centre of their thought but simply an objection which reinforced their primary denial and one which Paul could not ignore. But the primary doubt seems to have been over the subject of death, whether death had any further relevance to the fact of salvation.

To meet this questioning Paul reinforces the harsh reality of death; the familiar talk of death as a 'falling asleep' cannot hide the unavoidable conclusion that without a resurrection of the dead, the dead have perished (15.18). It would mean also that hope is confined to this life (15.19), with disastrous moral corollaries (15.30-34). In contrast Paul emphasizes that 'flesh and blood cannot inherit the kingdom of God' (15.50). But the core of his response is the twofold application of Adam Christology. First, that Christ's resurrection from the dead is a pattern for all, as had been Adam's death (15.20-23). And secondly, that the risen Christ has fulfilled God's original purpose for man/Adam in that all things have been put in subjection under his feet (15.27). The former meant that resurrection as resurrection of the dead was still to be experienced by believers. The latter is elaborated with the recognition that Christ's rule is not yet complete: not every ruler, authority and power has yet been destroyed, and the last enemy, death in particular, has still to be destroyed (15.24-27).

Apart from anything else, this reading of the text, or the variations in Lincoln and de Boer, indicate just how important the eschatological and apocalyptic dimension of the gospel was for Paul. Even if he makes some concession to a more dualistic (Greek) view of the material, in his distinction between the present natural body and the resurrected spiritual body (see above pp. 40-41), the fundamental structure of his thought is drawn primarily from Jewish apocalypticism. This also means that he is not troubled in recognizing the (continued) existence of many gods and lords and demons (8.6; 10.20-21), simply because, if they exist at all, they do so only within the framework of his apocalyptic schema, and under the sufferance of divine rule (15.25-28).

The Collection

A final brief mention should be made of 16.1-4 where Paul prefaces his travel plans by giving explicit instructions regarding the collection he was making 'for the saints' (16.1), that is, at Jerusalem (16.3). Whether this was one of the topics raised by the Corinthians (*peri de*) or at Paul's own behest, it is clear that the subject was familiar to the Corinthians, and that arrangements concerning its delivery were already well in hand. This confirms what is clear enough from elsewhere in the Pauline letters (Rom. 15.25-31; 2 Cor. 8-9; cf. Gal. 2.10), that the collection was an obligation of central importance for Paul, one for which he was willing to put his life in danger. Why this should be so is clear enough in broad outline, though not in detail. Fuller discussion of it belongs rather to the other two letters just mentioned. Here we need only note that Paul evidently saw it as a representative act of his churches (16.3-4). That the Jerusalem church was to be the sole beneficiary may tell us about the economic state of that church. But the more significant implication is that Paul saw it as a way of expressing Gentile Christian indebtedness to its Jewish heritage, as well as communion and concern between different churches, and probably a means of healing any breach between the mother church and the Gentile mission. One of the best treatments of the subject, that by Dieter Georgi, has recently been translated into English.

Within 1 Corinthians the significance accorded to the collection will depend in part on how strong a distinctively Jewish element or faction can be recognized in the church there. But whether we assess the specifically Jewish input to the tensions and factionalism in Corinth to be great or small, the significance of the collection as treated in 16.1-4 will remain: (a) that Paul should press such a Gentile-oriented church for contributions to far off Jerusalem, expecting them to share his concerns; (b) that they should apparently be so accepting of the obligation (the instructions are as to the *how* not the *why*); and (c) that Paul can make the request without any reference to the Corinthian factionalism, probably implying that he expected the well-to-do to provide (the bulk of) the collection for the church as a whole to send. Even if the strategy is in part at least to distract the Corinthians from their internal tensions by directing their sympathies to their more needy fellow-Christians elsewhere, the concern and its detailed practicality is impressive.

For Further Reading

R. Banks, *Paul's Idea of Community: The Early House Churches in their Historical Setting* (Exeter: Paternoster, 1980).

S.C. Barton, 'Paul's Sense of Place: an Anthropological Approach to Community Formation in Corinth', *NTS* 32 (1986), pp. 225-46.

S. Bedale, 'The Meaning of *kephalē* in the Pauline Epistles', *JTS* 5 (1954), pp. 211-15.

A. Bittlinger, Gifts and Graces (London: Hodder & Stoughton, 1967).

M.C. de Boer, *The Defeat of Death: Apocalyptic Eschatology in 1 Corinthians 15 and Romans 5* (Sheffield: JSOT Press, 1988).

T. Callan, 'Prophecy and Ecstasy in Greco-Roman Religion and in 1 Corinthians', *NovT* 27 (1985), pp. 125-40.

D.A. Carson, *Showing the Spirit: A Theological Exposition of 1 Corinthians 12–14* (Grand Rapids: Baker, 1987).

J.D.G. Dunn, *Jesus and the Spirit: A Study of the Religious and Charismatic Experience of Jesus and the First Christians as Reflected in the New Testament* (London: SCM Press/Philadelphia: Westminster Press, 1975).

E.S. Fiorenza, *In Memory of Her: A Feminist Theological Reconstruction of Christian Origins* (London: SCM Press, 1983).

J.A. Fitzmyer, 'Another Look at *kephalē* in 1 Corinthians 11.3', *NTS* 35 (1989), pp. 503-11.

D. Georgi, *Remembering the Poor: The History of Paul's Collection for Jerusalem* (Nashville: Abingdon, 1994).

D.W.J. Gill, 'In Search of the Social Elite in the Corinthian Church', *TynBul* 44 (1993), pp. 323-37.

W.A. Grudem, *The Gift of Prophecy in 1 Corinthians* (Washington, DC: University Press of America, 1982).

O. Hofius, 'The Lord's Supper and the Lord's Supper Tradition: Reflections on 1 Corinthians 11.23b-25', in B.F. Meyer (ed.), *One Loaf, One Cup: Ecumenical Studies of 1 Cor. 11 and Other Eucharistic Texts* (Macon, GA: Mercer University Press, 1993), pp. 75-115.

M.D. Hooker, 'Authority on her head: an examination of 1 Corinthians 11.10', *NTS* 10 (1964), reprinted in her *From Adam to Christ: Essays on Paul* (Cambridge: Cambridge University Press, 1990), pp. 113-20.

H.-J. Klauck, 'Presence in the Lord's Supper: 1 Corinthians 11.23-26 in the Context of Hellenistic Religious History', in Meyer (ed.), *One Loaf, One Cup*, pp. 57-74

H. Küng, *The Church* (London: Burns & Oates, 1968).

P. Lampe, 'The Eucharist: Identifying with Christ on the Cross', *Int* 48 (1994), pp. 36-49.

A.T. Lincoln, *Paradise Now and Not Yet: Studies in the Role of the Heavenly Dimension in Paul's Thought with Special Reference to Eschatology* (Cambridge: Cambridge University Press, 1981).

B.J. Malina, *The New Testament World: Insights from Cultural Anthropology* (London: SCM Press, 1983).

R.P. Martin, *The Spirit and the Congregation: Studies in 1 Corinthians 12–15* (Grand Rapids: Eerdmans, 1984).

J. Murphy-O'Connor, 'Sex and Logic in 1 Corinthians 11.2-16', *CBQ* 42 (1980), pp. 482-500.

T. Paige, '1 Corinthians 12.2: A Pagan Pompe?', *JSNT* 44 (1991), pp. 57-65.

E. Schweizer, *Church Order in the New Testament* (London: SCM Press, 1961).

G. Theissen, 'Social Integration and Sacramental Activity: An Analysis of 1 Cor. 11.17-34', in Theissen, *The Social Setting of Pauline Christianity* (Philadelphia: Fortress Press/Edinburgh: T. & T. Clark, 1982), ch. 4.

P. Trebilco, *Jewish Communities in Asia Minor* (Cambridge: Cambridge University Press, 1991).

A.C. Wire, *The Corinthian Women Prophets: A Reconstruction through Paul's Rhetoric* (Minneapolis: Fortress Press, 1990).

6

PAUL'S PASTORAL AND
THEOLOGICAL RESPONSE

WE HAVE NOW CLARIFIED, as far as is practically possible, the reasons why Paul felt it necessary to write as he did, what the issues were which he addressed, what the social context was in which they arose, whether and how the issues were related, and what they tell us about the church in Corinth itself. The picture which has emerged is confusing in detail but clear in overall outline. The church was quite small; the whole church could meet together in one place, that is, presumably, in the house of one of the more well-to-do members. There was a tendency to factionalism within the church, and for a variety of reasons: some were critical of Paul; some were acting in a high-handed way, confident in their knowledge and concerned more for personal advantage than communal good; and some of those of higher social status acted in disregard for their poorer brothers and sisters. There were tensions caused by changed status, when one or two of high social standing found themselves in relation to Paul both as potential patron to client and as child to father, or caught between their business or civic obligations and their new commitment, when only one partner in a marriage was baptized, or sexual relations were thought to conflict with dedication, and when wives became prophets, and charismatic enthusiasts allowed themselves to be carried away by their enthusiasm. There was disagreement about the significance of death.

This is an amazing diversity within a relatively small

group. No doubt several members were caught up in more than one of the issues. But attempts to see a single unified front behind every issue have not been noticeabley successful. Paul addresses the whole church, we may deduce, because the social tensions and factional tendencies were a problem for the church as a whole, and he wished them to be tackled with as common a will and mind as possible.

The question of *how* Paul hoped to meet this problem and what resources he was able to draw upon in doing so now arises. Some indication of *what* his answer was has already been given. Indeed, one of the principal reasons for spending so much time in clarifying the issue and context addressed in each case is that in so doing invaluable light is shed on Paul's teaching in response. A more detailed treatment of the 'what' would require a full scale commentary. But we can still say more on the 'how' and on the theological resources Paul was able to draw on. The first involves some consideration of Paul's pastoral strategy, and thus also of his ecclesiology. The other requires some reflection on the theology which underpins his answers.

Apostolic Power and Authority

It is obvious that the writing of 1 Corinthians was an attempt on Paul's part to exercise influence and authority in the life and affairs of the Corinthian church. It was in order to canvas his opinion and to draw from him such a statement that the letter had been written to him and Stephanas and the others had reported to him in the first place. Paul was evidently regarded, by the majority at least, as one whose advice and ruling should be sought on several controversial issues, as one who had a right to be consulted and to pronounce.

Paul for his part was in no doubt as to his responsibilities and rightful authority in reference to the Corinthian church. Thus he appeals to his apostleship on several occasions (1.1), not just as a status or vocation shared with others (4.9; 15.7, 9), but also as the Corinthians' apostle (founder of the church in Corinth, 9.1-2), and therefore as bearing a primacy of authority (12.28), which they above all ought to acknowledge (*exousia*—9.4-6, 12, 18). Hence also his exhortation in the thematic statement (1.10), where the verb (*parakaleō*) is in no sense a weak word (it is used, for example, in royal exhortation), his repeated appeal to his commission (1.17; 3.5-10; 4.1), his claim to exercise the power of the Spirit (2.4-5; 5.4; 7.40), his rebuke to them as a mature pneumatic speaking to 'people of the flesh, infants in Christ' (2.6-3.2), as their father (4.15), his assumption that he can serve as one to be imitated (4.16-17; 11.1), and his intolerance of dissent (4.18-21; 11.16; 14.37-38). We have already noted that Paul, although playing down the wisdom of speech, was not unskilled in rhetoric himself, so that his letter as an exercise in rhetoric is an attempt to persuade, and not simply to teach or rebuke (see above Chapters Two and Three, and Fiorenza below).

Before the recent re-emergence of rhetoric as a category to illuminate Paul's dealings with the Corinthians, they had proved amenable to a further application of sociological analysis. Max Weber had provided a valuable model which seemed to be of particular relevance to 1 Corinthians. This was the model of charismatic authority, an authority which derives from a prophet's immediate contact with the supernatural or sacred, and which brings disruption and innovation into the previous routine and institution, but whose transformation can only be sustained by itself being routinized or institutionalized. John Schütz was one of the first to apply Weber's understanding of charismatic authority to Paul, using a threefold distinction between power, authority and legitimacy, with power understood as the source of authority, authority as the application of power, and legitimacy as the formalization of authority. That such a model can be fitted quite readily to Paul's own exercise of authority is obvious. The more thoroughgoing use of Weber was that of Bengt Holmberg, though he drew upon it after he had analysed the distribution of power within the local Pauline churches and related Weber's model more to the relationship between Paul and Jerusalem. Margaret MacDonald in turn has analysed the early Pauline communities in terms of sect-formation, but her main interest is in the process of institutionalization.

On the most interesting issue for a study of 1 Corinthians
in particular, however, the discussion has not been very far
forwarded. That is the issue of how Paul understood his
apostolic authority in relation to the responsibilities of the
Corinthians themselves. To what extent did Paul genuinely
encourage his churches to exercise their own authority?
Hans von Campenhausen tried to demonstrate how careful
Paul was to circumscribe his own authority by the freedom of
his converts. Thus at various points Paul seems almost to fall
over backwards to encourage the Corinthians to take responsibility for themselves, even when the desirable course of
action is clear to him (5.3-5; 6.5), to avoid dictating policy
(7.25, 40) and allow as much space as possible for different
options (ch. 7), to concede and agree with catchwords which
were leading to actions of which he did not approve (ch. 8), to
plead freedom not to command rather than his rights as
apostle (ch. 9), to press the Corinthians to exercise a proper
discrimination in regard to spiritual gifts for themselves
(14.29), to argue with a different view on a crucial issue
rather than to pronounce against it (ch. 15). At times he
seems to lose patience and to speak in peremptory tone,
particularly once again 11.16 and 14.37-38, though in the
former case he seems somewhat embarrassed at having to
resort to that tone, and in the latter he expects the
Corinthians to recognize his instructions as the Lord's
command and to obey on that basis.

Against von Campenhausen, MacDonald (Part 1.2), among
others, has pointed to a degree of institutionalization already
present in the Corinthian church, in the mention of leaders
in 12.28 ('helpers and administrators') and in 16.15-18
(Stephanas, etc). Though it is doubtful whether the former
indicates formal ministries (the reference is more to acts
which help and provide guidance), and in the latter it is
noticeable that Paul has to push Stephanas and the others
forward for recognition by the rest.

Quite how the sociological analysis particularly of Chapter
Four above, fits in here is not entirely clear. Was the problem
that the social elite in the Corinthian church were indeed
providing leadership, but were using, in Paul's view, the
wrong model of leadership, dependent on social status and

rhetorical skill, as Clarke (above Chapter Four) has argued?
In contrast, the striking feature of 1 Corinthians is the lack
of any accepted or agreed leadership to whom Paul can
appeal to give a lead in any of the controversial issues he has
to deal with in the letter. The responsibility of the prophets
(12.28), for example, is related only to regulating the practice
of prophecy (14.29). Rather Paul's hope seems to be that the
Spirit will provide wisdom and leadership as needed (6.5;
12.8-10, 28-30), with the willingness of Stephanas and his
household to 'appoint themselves' to a ministry needing to be
done (16.15) perhaps serving as the model. Whether this
should nevertheless be described as a 'hierarchical leadership' (Clarke), or whether the Corinthian correspondence
demonstrates the unworkability of Paul's vision of 'charismatic community' (Dunn, *Jesus* [Chapter Five above], chs.
8–9) is another question.

Much fiercer is the critique of Graham Shaw, who sees
Paul's exercise of authority as blatantly manipulative, using
the 'language of freedom and reconciliation to clothe aggres-
sive self-aggression', his approach involving 'the pervasive
inculcation of bitterly divisive attitudes' (Shaw, pp. 181-83).
So, for example, in the case of 1 Cor. 5.3-5, 'the dichotomy in
Paul's mind between the body and the spirit gives a chari-
table veneer to exclusive and vindictive [a favourite Shaw
word] behaviour' (p. 70). Much of his response to the food
question is self-regarding, authoritarian and manipulative
(p. 85). 'The amount of practical diversity that the Pauline
church could tolerate was small' (p. 88). And more in the
same vein. Shaw's work is of interest as demonstrating how
far an unsympathetic reading or hermeneutic of suspicion
can go. Unfortunately he makes no real attempt to take
account of the historical context and social tensions in which
Paul was involved, and is so much at odds with the values
and beliefs of Paul and his correspondents ('That Christ was
raised to life anywhere other than in Paul's imagination is
unlikely' [p. 96]) that a positive appreciation of Paul was
more or less ruled out from the start.

A more credible assessment of Paul's strategy and one
which gathers together the different aspects of the various
current ways of analysing 1 Corinthians is that of Elisabeth

Schüssler Fiorenza. Sensitive to the rhetorical character of the letter and to the social factors in play at Corinth, she sees 1 Corinthians as a deliberative (persuasive) discourse appealing to those of higher social and educational status, but not including women of such status in this appeal.

A key passage in all this discussion has been ch. 9, particularly the famous 9.22, 'I have become all things to all, that I might by all means save some'. In a famous article, Henry Chadwick defends Paul against the charge that he was a weathercock and trimmer, and in effect against Shaw's charge that he was a manipulator. On the contrary, Paul demonstrates the skill of a good apologist: 'his astonishing ability to reduce to an apparent vanishing point the gulf between himself and his converts and to "gain" them for the Christian gospel', displaying 'an astonishing elasticity of mind, and a flexibility in dealing with situations requiring delicate and ingenious treatment which appears much greater than is usually supposed' (p. 275). Such a pastoral sensitivity combined with the rhetorical sophistication noted earlier seems closer to the Paul of 1 Corinthians than Shaw's picture of the vindictive manipulator (cf. also Mitchell in Chapter Two above). It need hardly be said, however, that one who expresses his principle in dealing with diverse and seemingly antithetical situations as Paul does in 9.19-23 inevitably leaves himself open to misunderstanding and misrepresentation. That is the character of the power and authority Paul sought to exert.

The passage has been extraordinarily fruitful in recent years, and we have already given it considerable attention in Chapter Four above. But two other recent essays make points worth noting. Barbara Hall reflects helpfully on Paul's attempt at radical identification with the other, weak as well as strong, in the face of Corinthian absorption with faction and self. The care with which Paul states his principle in 9.19-23 shows how Paul both safeguarded and expressed the essential freedom of the gospel precisely by this readiness to identify with different outworkings of the gospel. And Stephen Barton ('All Things') reminds us that the same formula is by no means only a 'missionary' principle, as is often assumed. Rather 'its primary connotation here is as a pastoral–political principle to do with compromise and self-denial for the sake of church unity'. The point is all the more significant given that the church in question was made up of people from a disconcertingly wide range of social backgrounds.

The Authority of Scripture

In attempting to persuade and to exercise authority and influence over the Corinthian church, what theological resources did Paul call upon? I will look at them in sequence; first, Scripture.

It is easy to forget (a) that the new movement was still understood as part of the diversity of first-century Judaism (it did not yet have a distinct, established identifying name), and (b) that its only authoritative documents were the Scriptures, that is, what Christians call the Old Testament. Precisely because it was understood as a messianic movement within Judaism, those who identified themselves with this new movement (through baptism in the name of Jesus) would recognize that the Scriptures of Israel were also their Scriptures and pay heed to them accordingly. Paul's regular reference to and use of these Scriptures, in 1 Corinthians as in most of his other letters, is thus wholly to be expected. For both Paul and his audience they were a source of authority with which his teaching and theirs had to be shown to accord.

In 1 Corinthians there are 13 quotations formally introduced as such (1.19, 31; 2.9; 3.19, 20; 6.16; 9.9, 10; 10.7; 14.21; 15.45, 54-55); though where 2.9b and 9.10 (but is 9.10 a quotation?) come from is entirely unclear. Christopher Stanley provides the most up to date discussion of the text forms cited. In the most interesting cases (3.19; 14.21; 15.45; 15.54-55) he concludes that in most cases the variations from the LXX should probably not be attributed to Paul but go back to his Greek version of the text cited, though several of the features in 14.21 are more likely to have been introduced by Paul himself and 15.55 was probably shaped by Paul. In addition there are five Scripture passages used by Paul but *not* formally introduced as such (2.16; 5.13; 10.26; 15.27;

15.32). This presumably tells us of a familiarity with the Scriptures which made them a natural part of Paul's thinking and speaking, just as well-read Shakespeare scholars might pepper their conversation with quotations from the bard.

Also noticeable are the number of allusions to and meditations on Scripture. A consultation of the margins of current Greek versions of the New Testament indicate the likelihood of many allusions. 5.7-8; 8.4; 9.13; 10.5, 18-22; 11.7-9; 14.25 and 15.25 are the most obvious. Again we gain the impression of a mind so steeped in the Scriptures that its language, images and stories actually shaped his thought. Earle Ellis argues that 2.6-16 and 10.1-13 were pre-shaped midrashim (expositions) which Paul has adapted to the present context. It looks also from 10.4 as though Paul was familiar with a Jewish midrash, on the rock from which Moses brought water in the wilderness, attested elsewhere not long after Paul in pseudo-Philo 10.7 and 11.15 (the water followed them in the wilderness 40 years). Ann Jervis argues that in 11.2-16 Paul has to correct the misunderstanding of his earlier exposition of the Genesis 1 creation account (man and woman being transformed into the image of the one who is beyond gender) by a midrashic combination of both creation accounts (Gen. 1 *and* 2), to indicate that their unity in Christ does not obliterate the diversity of the sexes. Paul's positive talk of 'keeping the commandments of God' in 7.19 should also be noted.

Most striking is the way Paul seems to draw his Christology from Scripture or to support it from Scripture. It was evidently important for Paul that the central claim of the gospel regarding Jesus' death and resurrection was 'in accordance with the Scriptures' (15.3-4). Several scholars (particularly Dunn, *Christology*) argue that 8.6 has been formulated on the basis of wisdom Christology, the agency in creation attributed to him being that of divine wisdom in Jewish wisdom tradition. What is notable is the way this Christology is integrated into Jewish monotheism ('for us there is one God') in effect by adapting the Jewish confession of God as one Lord (the Shema, Deut. 6.4; 1 Cor. 8.4). The implication of the earlier identification of Christ and Wisdom

in 1.24, 30 is that for Paul Christ crucified is now to be recog-
nized as the climax and definition of that wisdom by which
God made and orders the world. There is dispute, however,
as to whether 10.4 ('the rock was Christ') was intended by
Paul as a typological key to the mini-midrash in 10.1-4
(Dunn) or as an assertion of Christ's pre-existence as such
(Hanson).

Equally striking is the complementary Adam Christology
in 15.25-27 (merging Pss. 110.1 and 8.6) and 15.45-49 (elabo-
rating and expounding Gen. 2.7) (Dunn). Christ is understood as the eschatological equivalent to Adam, who, by his
exaltation as Lord, completes the original divine purpose in
creating Adam; that is, that Adam/humankind should have
dominion over 'all things'. Here again the way in which Paul
as a Jew integrates his understanding of Jesus as Lord
within his understanding of God as one and alone supreme
sovereign (15.28) is breathtaking in its boldness.

Finally the paraenetic use Paul makes of Scripture should
be noted. On the one hand he seems quite free to discount
circumcision and food laws (7.19; 10.25), despite their being
clearly defined as rules for the people of God in the
Scriptures. Yet at the same time he can claim that the
Scriptures were written for their (the Christians') benefit
(9.10; 10.11). Here, as in the christological usage, there is a
tension between recognition of the text as authoritative and
creative interpretation of that same text. In this way a new
tradition of understanding and using Scripture is developed
which at this stage is still part of the rich diversity of Jewish
usage of Scripture but is on the way to becoming something
distinctively Christian. Quite how creative use of Scripture
can function as a norm is a question which every generation
of Christianity has to wrestle with afresh.

The Authority of Jesus Tradition

1 Corinthians is also unique within the Pauline corpus in the
use it makes of the Jesus tradition, that is, the tradition
passed on within the earliest churches consisting of teach-
ings of Jesus and memories of his ministry. In other Pauline
letters it is not particularly obvious that Paul knew or made

much use of such tradition: there are no direct quotations from or references to it, and the number of plausible allusions is small. But in 1 Corinthians Paul explicitly cites a dominical tradition on no less than three occasions: 7.10 (Mk 10.11-12), 9.14 (Lk. 10.7//Mt. 10.10) and 11.23-26 (see below). David Dungan has devoted a monograph to the first two of these passages. He concludes that Paul stands squarely within the tradition that led to the Synoptic Gospels, and that he is conservative in his preservation of the tradition itself.

This latter point may need to be qualified since the third case (the Lord's Supper) is slightly different. Here we have a variation between the Mark/Matthew version of the 'words of institution' (Mt. 26.26-28//Mk 14.22-24) and those of Paul/Luke (1 Cor. 11.24-25//Lk. 22.19-20). But in addition we have indication of a developing liturgical tradition (the addition of the words, 'Do this in remembrance of me'). Paul also adds his own interpretative note in 11.26. Most notable of all is his attribution of the tradition to 'the Lord'. As Oscar Cullmann argued in a famous article ('The Tradition'), this seems to imply that Paul regarded the tradition as authoritative not just because it was tradition received through the earlier apostles, but because it was received on the direct authority of the exalted Christ.

Equally striking is Paul's treatment of the other two dominical utterances. In the first case it is notable that Paul again has to elaborate or go beyond the Lord's teaching on divorce to take account of the new circumstances confronting the Gentile churches (7.12-16). And in 9.14, despite his acknowledgment that 'the Lord commanded' evangelists to 'get their living from the gospel', Paul states bluntly that he sets aside his rights in this matter—that is, he ignores the Lord's command. The parallel with his treatment of Scripture is hard to deny. In both cases he clearly affirms the authority of what is cited. At the same time, however, he indicates that changed circumstances require some elaboration of the authoritative words or modification of the way their authority is applied. The authority as a living authority ('from the Lord') is experienced as such in context and in relation to context.

The question of why Paul does not cite more Jesus tradition has been debated frequently during the twentieth century. It may not be answered simply by pointing to the disputed number of allusions to Jesus tradition. The most plausible examples are clustered in the paraenetic sections of Romans 12–14 and 1 Thessalonians 5. In 1 Corinthians only 13.2 is widely recognized as an allusion to Jesus' saying about faith moving mountains (Mt. 17.20; 21.21//Mk 11.23). But it could be argued, for example, that the scandal of Jesus as Messiah in 1.23 reflects Mt. 11.6/Lk. 7.23, that the imagery of building wisely on a sure foundation 3.10-14 reflects Mt. 7.24-27//Lk. 6.47-49, and that Paul's talk of himself as a good steward (4.1-2) reflects Lk. 12.42. In an ambitious undertaking B. Fjärstedt has argued for the possibility that Paul's discussion of wisdom and foolishness in chs. 1–4 echoes the Q passage, Mt. 11.25-27//Lk. 10.21-22 (also Richardson), and that 9.1-14 shows the influence of Jesus' mission discourse (Mt. 10.1-10 with parallels). Nicholas Walter (p. 56) also points to a 'nest' of sayings in 4.11-12:

4.11a   Lk. 6.21a//Mt. 5.6; 10.9-10; 11.19
4.12b-13   Lk. 6.22-23//Mt. 5.11-12; Lk. 6.27-28.

However, as Walter also points out, in such sayings Paul shows no consciousness that he is citing Jesus tradition or interest in the question. Why should this be?

The answer can hardly be that the Jesus tradition was wholly unknown to Paul and his churches. That the first converts should not be interested in learning about Jesus defies human experience; or that the traditions later written down in the Synoptic Gospels were until then in a kind of limbo defies common sense. On the contrary, as Ellis points out, it is most likely that the apostles passed on such traditions as part of their church founding role. The letters are not the medium of such instruction, but rather can presuppose a knowledge of the Jesus tradition already transmitted. Such an apostolic activity is certainly indicated in references to Paul having passed on tradition (11.2, 23; 15.1, 3). Ellis argues further that the question posed in 10.16 ('The bread which we break, Is it not a participation in the body of Christ?') presupposes instruction on Jesus' words at the last supper so that Paul could expect an answer. The other references to 'body of Christ' theology (6.15; 12.12, 27) strengthen the suggestion that this was a subject of earlier apostolic teaching. But still the question persists, Why then is Jesus not explicitly cited as authority in such cases?

Alexander Wedderburn (p. 100) has suggested that Paul might be hesitant to do so because the Jesus tradition was largely 'in enemy hands', by which he means the Jerusalem based missionaries opposed to Paul. Dunn's alternative is that the manner of allusion to the Jesus tradition is precisely what we should expect among communities whose common identity was constituted in large part by the tradition they shared. Part of the 'glue' which bonds a community together will be its shared discourse, traditions and language which can be taken for granted by members of the community, the 'in-jokes' and coded references which facilitate communication between members and prevent outsiders from following the exchanges. In such a case it is the allusiveness of the reference which forms the 'glue'; to spell out the reference and its source would break the code and loosen the bond, since anyone could now appreciate the point. In contrast, it is presumably significant that in the two cases where Paul cites a word from the Lord, he does so in order to elaborate or qualify it. He only cites it because he is qualifying it, whereas the allusion implies an accepted authority. Ironically, then, the authority of such allusions to the shared Jesus tradition was strengthened (for those who recognised the allusion) rather than diminished (as being 'only an allusion').

It is to be noted once again, however, that the authority of an allusion functions differently from that of an explicit quotation where the authoritative source is also cited. The authority of allusion does not rest solely in itself, in the words used. It depends more on its effectiveness as an allusion. That is to say, it depends also on its character as shared discourse, on its social and communal function, on the sense of community which the allusion expresses and to which it appeals. Here again, in other words, authority cannot be absolutized or abstracted but functions contextually. At the same time, there was a sufficiently coherent and regular pattern of community and ethical life emerging from this shared tradition so that Paul could appeal on several occasions to this common practice (4.17; 7.17; 11.16; 14.33) as an important factor to be weighed in resolving matters of local dispute (see further Tomson).

Finally it is important to note that all the citations and allusions to Jesus tradition refer to ethical teaching or to praxis (liturgical or missiological). This is presumably why 1 Corinthians, the letter of Paul most devoted to practical issues, is so unusual in the number of direct quotations. In contrast, 'It is precisely in his decisive theological statements that Paul adduces no Jesus-tradition' (Walter, p. 63). Again we must ask, Why so? The answer is partly that the gospel, Paul's central theological affirmation, is focused more on Jesus' death and resurrection, as we shall see in a moment. But bound up in the issue is the further question of how much Jesus' life, the character of his ministry and not just his teaching, was part of the Jesus tradition. This is not a question which can really be answered from 1 Corinthians, again primarily because of the scope of its subject matter. It hangs more on passages like Rom. 15.1-5 and Gal. 6.2, and on whether Paul's openness to Gentile 'sinners' reflected a tradition of Jesus who 'came to call sinners' (Mark 2.17) (see Dunn 168-72). At most in 1 Corinthians 9.21 can be cited ('in-lawed to Christ', or 'under Christ's law'), on which C.H. Dodd wrote a famous article, and 11.1 ('Be imitators of me, as I am of Christ').

The Authority of the Gospel

Not least of 1 Corinthians' riches is the fact that it includes 15.3-8. Here is Paul's own statement of the gospel which he had proclaimed to the Corinthians and which was the means of their salvation ('through which you also are being saved') (15.1-2). Not only so, but Paul tells/reminds them that this is the very gospel which he himself also had received. By common consent Paul refers back to his own conversion, which must take us back to within two or three years of the events referred to therein (Christ's death and resurrection). In other words, here we have a first-hand account (and not just Luke's second- or third-hand account written down half a century later) of what the gospel was and how it was being formulated already within two or three years of Christianity's beginnings.

The focus of the gospel is clear:

> that Christ died for our sins in accordance with the Scriptures,
> and that he was buried
> and that he was raised on the third day in accordance with the Scriptures,
> and that he appeared to Cephas,
> then to the twelve,
> then he appeared to over five hundred brothers.

This accepted tradition clearly forms the basis for Paul's full scale teaching on the resurrection of the dead which is the subject of the chapter (see above pp. 84-87). Its centrality to Paul's whole understanding of the gospel is clearly indicated in 15.14 and 17.

As with the Jesus tradition, there seem to be several allusions to the gospel as thus defined in Paul's letters. They appear typically in relative clauses, in what might be called liturgical echoes. In 1 Corinthians we may note the repeated theme, 'God raised the Lord/Christ' (6.14; 15.12, 20), the more typical, 'on account of whom Christ died' (8.11), and the untypical 'Christ our paschal lamb has been sacrificed' (5.7) and 'You were bought with a price' (6.20; 7.23). Not much original work has been done on these formulae since Werner Kramer's still important study. But we can confidently draw the same conclusion as in the last section: these allusions added to the evidence of 15.1-8, clearly indicate (a) that the death and resurrection of Jesus was at the heart of the gospel, (b) that churches like the one in Corinth were thoroughly schooled in that central affirmation, (c) and that this affirmation was regularly reinforced by allusions to it, (d) so that allusions like this would have been recognized as invoking the central claim of the gospel.

In terms of effective authority these allusions are crucial in providing the basis for Paul's theological affirmation in 15.12 and 20 and for his practical teaching in 5.7; 6.14, 20; 7.23 and 8.11. The formula in 12.3, 'Jesus is Lord', seems to function in a similar way. It is the test of valid inspiration, presumably in that it sums up, in confessional form, the

character as well as claim of the gospel. Other references to
the gospel confirm its vital function for Paul: he brought
them to birth through it (4.15); hence his total commitment
to his commission to preach it, overriding other concerns and
claims (1.17; 9.12-23). As Schütz pointed out, Paul did not
see his authority as apostle as independent of the gospel: on
the contrary it was authorization to preach the gospel and
was subordinate to the gospel.

In this connection, 1.17–2.5 is particularly noticeable. Here
it is the term *kerygma* ('proclamation', 1.21; 2.4; 15.14) which
predominates rather than 'gospel' (*euangelion*). This is
because in the context of chs. 1–2 the emphasis is on the
preaching of the gospel. What is striking is the way Paul
brings all the disputed issues, focused round the theme of
wisdom, to the touchstone of the message proclaimed: 'Christ
crucified' (1.13, 17-18, 23; 2.2). Astonishingly and paradoxi-
cally the cross is the measure of God's wisdom which under-
mines the values and priorities of human wisdom. Since
crucifixion was regarded as the most shameful of deaths the
transformation and reversal of normal social and moral
values could not have been more striking or have been
missed by Paul's correspondents. Those who made Christ
crucified their standard thereby opted for an alternative
value system which (should have!) turned upside down
customary notions of honour and shame and prestige (see
e.g. Barton, 'Cross'). Hence this should also be the yardstick
by which they measured their own responsibilities towards
one another (8.11), the model for their own conduct as it was
for Paul (4.11-13; 11.1).

Nor should we forget that the significance and authoritative effect of the eucharistic tradition cited in 11.23-26
focuses on the death of Christ (cf. 10.16) and is regarded by
Paul as a proclamation of the Lord's death until he comes.
Given the recognition in Chapter Five that the frictions
addressed in 11.17-34 are social rather than theological, it is
again all the more striking that Paul addresses these social
problems with an essentially theological argument. As
Otfried Hofius observes (see above Chapter Five), 'the table
of the Lord' cannot be a private affair, where each might do
as he pleases. On the contrary, the liturgically preserved

tradition of Jesus' last supper and the significance it puts upon his death is what determines the character of the coming together for the shared meal. It is the 'for you' character of Jesus' action (11.24) which should bind the community together in mutual responsibility one for another, transcending all social differences (Hofius, p. 113).

This also explains why 'love' (*agape*) is such an important criterion for church life and relationships—presumably because it is the love which Christ himself expressed, and most clearly on the cross. Like the wisdom of the cross, love brings a different system of values and order of reality to bear on the present (13.8, 13). It is notable then that Paul appeals to it as the check against abuse of liberty (8.1), that the great chapter of love functions as the key criterion of the value of charisms, faith, knowledge and even self-sacrifice (13.1–14.1), and that Paul can sum up all his counsel to the Corinthians in the single summary injunction, 'Let all that you do be done in love' (16.14), answering to the thematic concern of 1.10 (Mitchell, p. 94 n. 170; see above Chapter Two). Clearly conjoint with love is the other criterion which Paul uses to direct the expression of liberty (8.1, 10; 10.23, 33) and to assess the relative merit of different charisms (14.3-5, 12, 17), namely, *oikodomē* or   community benefit, what builds up the church; it too can provide a summary norm, in this case for congregational worship (14.26).

Also integral to the gospel of Jesus Christ is the eschatological perspective. Most striking is the sense of what is usually described as 'realized eschatology'—the sense that a new age has dawned, as attested not least by the outpouring of the Spirit; and not just a new age, but *the* new age, the final stage of God's purpose. This is implicit in the contrast with 'this age' which runs through chs. 1–3 (1.20; 2.6-8; 3.18), clearer in 7.31 (the form of this age is passing away) and 10.11 (believers as those 'upon whom the end of the ages has come'), and most explicit in the imagery of Christ's resurrection as the 'first fruits' (that is, beginning of the harvest) of the resurrection from the dead (15.20-23). It has already been established that this was a factor in the problems at Corinth, that is, an overemphasis on what they had already received (as indicated most sharply in 4.8).

In contrast, Paul also emphasizes the not yet aspect of eschatology: they await the revealing of the Lord Jesus Christ (1.7; 10.16), they are in process of being saved (1.18; 15.2), the kingdom of God is still to be inherited (6.9-10; 15.50), their vision and knowledge is still imperfect (13.9-13), not forgetting the whole extensive argument of ch. 15, together with the concluding 'Maranatha, Our Lord come' (16.22). Particularly important here as a warning to the Corinthians is the emphasis on future judgment (especially 3.10–4.5). In the most recent study of the passage, David Kuck argues that Paul did not have to convince the Corinthians of the reality of future judgment as a counter to over-realized eschatology; even 4.8 is addressed to ethical rather than eschatological overconfidence. Instead, Paul is using the symbolic language of future judgment in order to resolve the tensions in Corinth caused by individuals seeking status in the church (p. 222). Whether he is right on this, the crucial element for us here again is that Christ (and by implication the gospel focused in Christ) is the one foundation which will be sufficient to endure that final searching scrutiny by fire (3.10-15).

Much more could be said on this theme of the authority of the gospel, since it in fact provides the foundation for and determines the character of Paul's theology as a whole. But space begins to press, and there have been two recent summary treatments of Paul's theology in 1 Corinthians as such (Fee and Furnish). It must suffice to make one final brief note.

As a final theological reflection, it is not unimportant to note how the gospel of Christ crucified and exalted as Lord functions as the lynchpin of a redefinition of the ultimate authority, God. As already noted, God in his wisdom, as creator and revealer, is now defined by reference to the cross, just as the the *Shema* is redefined by incorporating reference to the same Christ (1.23-24; 8.4-6). In a similar way, the Spirit of God is now understood as that power which brings conviction through the *kerygma* and which inspires the confession of Jesus' Lordship (2.2-4; 12.3). It is not that Christ supplants God or the Spirit. Far from it: God is still the power behind the gospel (1.18–2.16), and the Spirit is still the Spirit of God (2.10-14; 3.16; 6.11; 7.40; 12.3); Christ is still under God (3.23; 11.3) and God is still one (8.6) and the ultimate (15.24-28). Rather it is the correlation between Christ proclaimed, and the God of Scripture on the one hand and the charismatic impact of the Spirit on the other, which both required and confirmed for Paul the reconstruction of his ancestral faith into what was to become a Trinitarian form.

For Further Reading

S.C. Barton, 'Paul and the Cross: A Sociological Approach', *Theology* 85 (1982), pp. 13-19.

—' "All Things to All People": Paul and the Law in the Light of 1 Corinthians 9.19-23', in J.D.G. Dunn (ed.), *Paul and the Law* (Tübingen: Mohr, 1996).

H. von Campenhausen, *Ecclesiastical Authority and Spiritual Power in the Church of the First Three Centuries* (London: A. & C. Black, 1969).

H. Chadwick, ' "All Things to All Men" (1 Cor. 9.22)', *NTS* 1 (1954–55), pp. 261-75.

O. Cullmann, 'The Tradition', in *The Early Church: Historical and Theological Studies* (London: SCM Press, 1956), pp. 59-75.

C.H. Dodd, *'Ennomos Christou'*, in *More New Testament Studies* (Manchester: Manchester University Press, 1968), pp. 134-48.

D.L. Dungan, *The Sayings of Jesus in the Churches of Paul: The Use of the Synoptic Tradition in the Regulation of Early Church Life* (Oxford: Basil Blackwell, 1971).

J.D.G. Dunn, *Christology in the Making: An Inquiry into the Origins of the Doctrine of the Incarnation* (London: SCM Press, 2nd edn, 1989)

—'Jesus Tradition in Paul', in B. Chilton and C. A. Evans (eds.), *Studying the Historical Jesus: Evaluations of the State of Current Research* (Leiden: Brill, 1994), pp. 155-78.

E.E. Ellis, 'Traditions in 1 Corinthians', *NTS* 32 (1986), pp. 481-502.

G.D. Fee, 'Toward a Theology of 1 Corinthians', in D. M. Hay (ed.), *Pauline Theology*. II. *1 & 2 Corinthians* (Minneapolis: Fortress Press, 1993), pp. 37-58.

E.S. Fiorenza, 'Rhetorical Situation and Historical Reconstruction in 1 Corinthians', *NTS* 33 (1987), pp. 386-403.

B. Fjärstedt, *Synoptic Tradition in 1 Corinthians: Themes and Clusters of Theme Words in 1 Corinthians 1–4 and 9* (Uppsala: Lundeqvist, 1974).

V.P. Furnish, 'Theology in 1 Corinthians', in Hay *Pauline Theology*. II. *1 & 2 Corinthians*, pp. 59-89.

B. Hall, 'All Things to All People: A Study of 1 Corinthians 9.19-23', in R.T. Fortna and B.R. Gaventa (eds.), *The Conversation Continues: Studies in Paul and John: In Honor of J.L.Martyn* (Nashville: Abingdon, 1990), pp. 137-57.

A.T. Hanson, *The Image of the Invisible God* (London: SCM Press, 1982), ch. 4.

B. Holmberg, *Paul and Power: the Structure of Authority in the Primitive Church as Reflected in the Pauline Epistles* (Lund: Gleerup, 1978).

L.A. Jervis, ' "But I want you to know...": Paul's Midrashic Intertextual Response to the Corinthian Worshippers (1 Cor. 11.2-16)', *JBL* 112 (1993), pp. 231-46.

W. Kramer, *Christ, Lord, Son of God* (London: SCM Press, 1966).

D.W. Kuck, *Judgment and Community Conflict: Paul's Use of Apocalyptic Judgment Language in 1 Corinthians 3.5–4.5* (NovTSup, 66; Leiden: Brill, 1992).

M.Y. MacDonald, *The Pauline Churches: A Socio-historical Study of Institutionalization in the Pauline and Deutero-Pauline Writings* (Cambridge: Cambridge University Press, 1988).

P. Richardson, 'The Thunderbolt in Q and the Wise Man in Corinth', in P. Richardson and J.C. Hurd (eds.), *From Jesus to Paul: Studies in Honour of F.W. Beare* (Waterloo, Ontario: Wilfrid Laurier University Press, 1984), pp. 91-111.

J.H. Schütz, *Paul and the Anatomy of Apostolic Authority* (Cambridge: Cambridge University Press, 1975).

G. Shaw, *The Cost of Authority: Manipulation and Freedom in the New Testament* (London: SCM Press, 1983).

C.D. Stanley, *Paul and the Language of Scripture: Citation Technique in the Pauline Epistles and Contemporary Literature* (Cambridge: Cambridge University Press, 1992).

P.J. Tomson, *Paul and the Jewish Law: Halakha in the Letters of the Apostle to the Gentiles* (Assen: Van Gorcum/Minneapolis: Fortress Press, 1990).

N. Walter, 'Paul and the Early Christian Jesus-Tradition', in Wedderburn, *Paul and Jesus*, pp. 51-80.

A.J.M. Wedderburn, *Paul and Jesus: Collected Essays* (JSNTSup, 37; Sheffield: JSOT Press, 1989), includes his own essay, 'Paul and Jesus: Similarity and Continuity', pp. 99-115.

7

CONCLUSION

WHERE DOES ALL THIS LEAVE US? What difference does it make
that we can find some archaeological evidence which ties in
with some detail or other in the letter? Does it matter
whether we can define the letter as deliberative or persuasive in its rhetoric? Why should it concern us whether there
was one or more parties in the Corinthian church, whether
there was Gnostic or Hellenistic Jewish influence, political
style factionalism or over-enthusiastic spirituality? Does it
make any difference to the way we read the letter that there
were social tensions between rich and poor, patrons and
clients, high status and low, husbands and wives? Is the
confusion occasioned when the Corinthian Christians came
together for worship or the idiosyncracy of their 'zeal for
spirits' something that should affect us? And does it matter
whether we can decide that Paul's handling of these problems was pastorally sensitive or politically manipulative,
inspired by love or authoritarian in character?

As the Introduction already indicated, the answer to these
questions can, for the most part, be positive and without
embarrassment. As a matter of historical responsibility it is
important to gain as clear as possible a perspective on the
situation of the church in Corinth and on Paul's handling of
it. It is all too easy, whether by way of idealizing the earliest
churches, or by way of reacting against such idealization, to
misrepresent even the facts as we have them. It is important,
for example, that we can see earliest Christianity, at least as
represented by the church in Corinth, not simply as the
prerogative of the well-to-do or alternatively as 'the opium of

the masses', and not as a movement which shut itself off from the wider world in an other-worldly spirituality. It is important that we do not allow either a theological or a sociological or a literary reductionism to determine our reading of the text, but recognize both the social dimensions of the theology and the theological constraints on the social interaction, as well as the dynamic of spiritual experience interacting with rhetorical art.

Here in 1 Corinthians we see, perhaps more clearly than anywhere else, the impact of the Christian message and experience in process of working their effect in one of the formative periods for the history and culture of modern Europe. That we can also see these effects outworking in the lives of real people, caught up in social and theological tensions in ways which we today can recognize without too much difficulty, gives us a more realistic appreciation of what that message and experience amounted to. And that these effects were no easy panacea but had to be worked through by and in community with people who found it difficult to get on with each other is perhaps the most salutary lesson of all. For despite all that, the letter intended to meet these concerns worked its own power. Not that it resolved all the problems and tensions—far from it. But it provided an anchor and touchstone for faith outworking in conduct and corporate worship maintained despite social tension, which the Corinthians evidently treasured, despite Paul's rebukes, and which was thus preserved to become a resource for churches thereafter.

Not of least significance is the picture of Paul himself which emerges from this study, and precisely in his capacity as both theologian and missionary-pastor. For we have seen repeatedly how Paul brought theological principles and convictions to bear on what were characteristically social issues, and how the gospel provided criteria and norms for questions of ethical conduct and community responsibility. But we have also seen, and consistently from Chapter Six, how ready Paul was to exercise this authority in the light of the circumstances he addressed. This emerges not simply from his stated principle of missionary and pastoral strategy—'all things to all people' (9.22). It also becomes apparent in the way Paul not only used but also elaborated and qualified the authority of Scripture, of the Jesus tradition and even of the gospel itself. He was neither simply a creative theologian, 'making it up as he went along'; nor simply an authoritarian pastor routinely following rules and rubrics. The word for him was not a crystallized deposit, but a living expression of the shared experience of Spirit and the fellowship of commitment. The tradition maintained the continuity with the past of Israel and the past of Jesus. The gospel remained focused on the cross and resurrection of Christ. But its expression in teaching and exhortation, rebuke and challenge, spoke to the Corinthians in the midst of the complex demands of their lives and relationships and with an astonishing relevancy and effect. In this aspect also 1 Corinthians can still be a model and resource.

INDEXES

INDEX OF REFERENCES

INDEX OF AUTHORS